Picture me doing the deliberately slow appreciation clap while I read this book. The topic of students engaging in ministry—especially the ministry of influence—is one of my own passions, so I approached this book ready to wrangle over values and strategies. Instead, I find myself in jealous admiration for how well these guys have translated important principles into practical tips so church youth leaders can experience the joyous fruit of *Ministry by Teenagers*.

—Dave Rahn
Senior VP & Chief Ministry Officer, Youth for Christ/USA
Coauthor, *Evangelism Remixed: Empowering Students for Courageous and Contagious Faith*

For too long, youth ministry has treated the term *teenage leadership* as an oxymoron. Rather than empowering young people to join us in leadership, we warehouse them until they are old enough to leave, which is exactly what many of them do. This book is a welcome antidote. Jonathan and David believe in teenagers and have given us a solid strategy for discovering, developing, and deploying the considerable gifts and capabilities of today's young people.

—Wayne Rice
Cofounder of Youth Specialties; founder, Understanding Your Teenager seminars

Without even knowing it, we sometimes expect far too little from our students. The result is missed opportunities to lead students to a deeper lifelong potential. Jonathan and David have given us a helpful and practical guide to make this happen. Don't miss the opportunity!

—Dr. Walt Mueller
President, Center for Parent/Youth Understanding

Ministry by Teenagers is a must-read for every youth leader serious about unleashing teenagers to do more than just show up, sit down, and shut up. This book is for those who, like Jesus, want to mobilize disciples for significant (not token) kingdom action. Jonathan McKee and David R. Smith provide easy-to-apply strategies, practical examples, and rock-solid biblical truth.

—Greg Stier
President, Dare 2 Share Ministries
Author of *Venti Jesus Please* and *Dare 2 Share: A Field Guide t*

Jonathan McKee and David R. Smith have constructed an effective guide to move beyond programs "to" youth and develop youth ministry done "by" youth. They champion the historic role of student leadership that has faded in recent years, but remains a necessary value for effective youth ministry. They provide easy-to-follow guidelines and outlines that will help you take the next step in developing your teens into leaders.

—Terry Linhart
Author and Teacher
Bethel College, Indiana

This is one of the most practical youth ministry books on developing disciples and encouraging leadership in kids. It is a great addition to anyone's youth ministry library.

—Jim Burns, PhD
President, HomeWord
Author of *Teenology, Confident Parenting*, and *The Purity Code*

Ministry by Teenagers offers biblically sound, practical, easy-to-follow, step-by-step advice on developing true student disciples of Jesus. Jonathan and David flesh this out with real-life stories, evaluative tools, and helpful forms. Taking the principles from this book will put you on the path to developing in each of your students a faith that lasts a lifetime. Jonathan and David carefully address major concerns when equipping student servant leaders. Our job as youth workers is to bring students to maturity in Christ (Col. 1:28) and prepare them for some form of ministry (Eph. 4:12). This book will help you develop the leadership potential that exists in every student and help you follow Jesus' leadership standard, "He that is greatest among you shall be your servant." I highly recommend it.

—Les Christie
Chair, Youth Ministry Department, William Jessup University
Author of *When Church Kids Go Bad*

MINISTRY BY TEENAGERS

DEVELOPING LEADERS FROM WITHIN

JONATHAN MCKEE
& DAVID R. SMITH

 youth specialties

ZONDERVAN.com/
AUTHORTRACKER
follow your favorite authors

ZONDERVAN

Ministry by Teenagers
Copyright © 2011 by Jonathan McKee and David R. Smith

YS Youth Specialties is a trademark of YOUTHWORKS!, INCORPORATED and is registered with the United States Patent and Trademark Office.

This title is also available as a Zondervan ebook. Visit www.zondervan.com/ebooks.

Requests for information should be addressed to:

Zondervan, *Grand Rapids, Michigan 49530*

Library of Congress Cataloging-in-Publication Data

McKee, Jonathan R. (Jonathan Ray), 1970 –
     Ministry by teenagers : developing leaders from within / Jonathan McKee and David R. Smith..
       p. cm.
     ISBN 978-0-310-67077-3 (softcover)
     1. Church work with teenagers. 2. Christian leadership. I. Smith, David R., 1977- II. Title.
   BV4447.M35 2010
   253.0835—dc22
                                         20010043474

All Scripture quotations, unless otherwise indicated, are taken from the Holy Bible, *Today's New International Version™. TNIV®.* Copyright 2001, 2005 by Biblica, Inc.™ Used by permission of Zondervan. All rights reserved worldwide.

Scripture quotations marked NIV are taken from the Holy Bible, *New International Version®, NIV®.* Copyright © 1973, 1978, 1984 by Biblica, Inc.™ Used by permission of Zondervan. All rights reserved worldwide.

Any Internet addresses (websites, blogs, etc.) and telephone numbers printed in this book are offered as a resource. They are not intended in any way to be or imply an endorsement by Zondervan, nor does Zondervan vouch for the content of these sites and numbers for the life of this book.

Cover design: IMAGO
Interior design: David Conn

Printed in the United States of America

CONTENTS

MORE THAN DODGEBALL
DO WE EVEN NEED TEENAGE LEADERSHIP?

A few years ago I (Jonathan) met a young girl at my church named Heather. During Heather's eighth-grade year, she introduced five of her school friends to Jesus.

Five friends!

How many of *your friends* have you introduced to Jesus this year?

Yeah, Heather has me beat, too.

Those five friends, all girls, brought even more friends to youth group. My wife and I helped in the youth group at the time. So my wife began discipling Heather and several others in this growing group of girls. About eight of them became regulars at our church.

It doesn't take a rocket scientist to figure out what happens when eight cute girls start going to church.

Yup. Guys started coming to church—guys who'd never even thought about church before.

By the end of Heather's eighth-grade year, about 10 to 15 of her friends were regular attendees—and seven gave their lives to Jesus. Several of them went off to Christian colleges after high school. One was Heather's college roommate at Point Loma Nazarene University.

For many youth workers, 15 kids is an entire youth group. For Heather 15 kids was the result of her heart to see her non-Christian friends find hope in their lives. Wouldn't it be cool to have a Heather in every church?

Aaron was the first person to greet me when I (Jonathan) walked into the youth ministry office at a small church in the Bible Belt. A youth pastor from the church, named Brian, had contacted me a few months prior and booked me to come speak and train for the weekend.

Aaron asked about my flight, and we made small talk for a few minutes. I quickly discovered Brian wasn't even there—he was out running errands. No worries. Aaron was warm and engaging.

"We've been praying about this weekend for a long time," Aaron offered. "We're really excited for what God has planned."

Aaron and I talked about the plans for the weekend as he stapled some packets together. Brian and I had gone over the schedule multiple times, but it was interesting to hear Aaron's perspective and expectations for the weekend. (I'm always intrigued to hear what's been communicated to other leaders in the ministry.)

"Do you see the focus of this weekend as outreach or spiritual growth?" I asked Aaron.

Aaron arranged a small stack of papers on the counter and then rested his hands for a moment, pondering the question. "I think we're starting with more of an outreach focus, but then we'll slowly move toward spiritual growth."

I nodded in agreement, setting down my laptop bag and leaning on the desk to my right.

"Tonight all the kids are bringing their friends," he continued, "and you'll present the gospel. That's outreach. But it's also a step of growth for many of the kids because they've been praying for this night for a long time, and they've each invited friends they've been praying for."

Aaron picked up one of the stapled packets for me to see. "Tomorrow morning you'll train the leadership team with your workshop. That's also an opportunity for spiritual growth as we'll learn how to do better ministry." He placed the packet neatly in the pile with the others. "And finally, on Sunday morning I think your preaching in the services will focus on helping the congregation grow as well." He raised his eyebrows and shrugged his shoulders. "Right?"

I smiled. "I think that's the plan."

Brian, the youth pastor who was still AWOL, had verbalized the weekend's focus to me several times over the phone. But his assistant, Aaron, had articulated it better than I'd heard yet.

I was helping Aaron staple the remaining packets when Brian finally arrived, apologetic about getting stuck in a department store line.

An hour later Brian and I were sitting in a restaurant dialoguing about the weekend while Aaron ran a few errands. I mentioned that Aaron had gone over the schedule with me a little bit. "He's a sharp guy," I added.

"Aaron?" Brian clarified, stirring his milkshake with a spoon. "Oh man! Absolutely. We're blessed to have Aaron."

I realized I'd never learned Aaron's role in the youth ministry. So I asked, "Is Aaron your middle school director? Your intern?" Youth ministries have so many staff positions these days; it's hard to know who's filling which roles.

Brian stopped stirring his shake and looked at me with a blank expression on his face. "Aaron?"

For a second I wondered if my question had confused him.

Brian cracked a smile. "Aaron's in eleventh grade. He's one of my student leaders."

I was shocked. "St . . . st . . . student? Aaron's a student?"

Brian chuckled, "Has been since kindergarten." He took a sip of his milkshake. "Of course, I didn't have him until middle school. He wasn't a perfect kid, but he was always hungry for truth, and he found it in the Bible. I've been discipling him since eighth grade. Last year—his sophomore year—Aaron joined our teen leadership team. He's moved from attending Bible studies to leading them."

"Wow," I finally offered. "Aaron sounds like a real asset to your ministry."

"Jonathan," he said, leaning in really close, "you have no idea. If I'm going to be out of town on Sunday, I don't call any of my adult leaders . . . I call Aaron."

"Wow!" I repeated, at a loss for words. What I was honestly thinking was, *I want an Aaron!*

Don't you?

Heather—a kid who did more outreach in a year than most youth workers do in a career.

Aaron—a kid who could run a Bible study . . . or the entire youth group . . . by himself.

Forget about all our programs and ministry methodologies for a moment. Set aside all our volunteer training and development, as important as that is, for just a moment. Can you imagine if your ministry had a "Heather" and an "Aaron"? What about a few "Heathers" and "Aarons"?

Think about how our ministries could be radically transformed with teen leaders like these two.

Now let me ask you a more probing question: How much time are you devoting to developing "Heathers" and "Aarons"?

DEVELOPING DISCIPLES

When Jesus finished his ministry on earth, his last words before he returned to the heavens were hard to forget: "Go and make disciples" (Matthew 28:19). How many of us are really doing that?

Let me quickly clarify: Discipling a kid doesn't make that kid a leader. But in the case of Jesus and his disciples, numerous leaders did emerge, including Peter, who became "the rock" on which Jesus built his church.

It all started with discipleship.

Recently, our ministry surveyed thousands of youth workers who use the free resources on our website, asking them how these tools and resources have helped them. We asked them a handful of questions, including these two:

• Have these resources helped you introduce teens to Jesus?
• Have these resources helped your teens grow spiritually?

I was amazed at how many people didn't even address those questions.

Allow me to explain. This isn't due to a lack of these kinds of resources on our ministry's website. Our front page alone contains an "Outreach Resource of the Week" and "Spiritual Growth Resource of the Week." The focus of our ministry is helping youth workers make an eternal impact. Our site is content-rich.

Regardless, most youth workers who responded thanked us for the games and skits our site provides. The majority didn't even answer the questions about their kids meeting Jesus or growing spiritually. Some candid responses were, "Our program is going great; but no, I don't think I've seen much of those two things" ("those two things" being *meeting Jesus* and *growing spiritually*).

Think about that statement for a second: "Our program is going great . . ." I'd be curious to know their definition of *great*.

Does *great* mean big numbers? Maybe it means large numbers of ice-cream sundaes consumed? Perhaps *great* means a huge response to the dodgeball tournament?

How great are our youth ministries if we "aren't seeing much" of kids putting their trust in Jesus or growing spiritually?

As our ministry's content team got together to review the survey results, our jaws dropped at some of the responses we received from youth workers around the world. (We sent our survey to thousands and received hundreds of responses.) We saw it again and again: "Thanks for the games! We use them every week!"

I'd read a response like that and yell, "AND . . . ?" (There's no denying that I'm a dramatic person.)

I'm fine with games if they help connect us with kids or break down walls between us and them. But what then? I wanted to scream, "What are you doing to make a lasting impact with teenagers? What are you doing to expose kids to the truth from the Word of God?"

Will playing dodgeball, attending Christian rock concerts, and participating in icebreakers be the only youth ministry experiences our kids have to lean on when they face the real world? Or are those activities opening doors to something more foundational for their lives?

Yesterday (as I write this) I looked at our web statistics to examine the traffic on our website—something I try to do once a month. Do you know what the top two pages were?

"Games" and "Skits."

Imagine our disappointment.

If you're like us, you want to make an eternal impact in the lives of teenagers—not just break the record for the most marshmallows shoved into a kid's mouth.

I don't think many youth workers would argue against God's desire for us to "Go and make disciples"! The question is, "Are we really making disciples, or are we just making a lot of root beer floats?"

The question is, "Are we really making disciples, or are we just making a lot of root beer floats?"

And we wonder why kids are exiting their faith when they leave high school.

What are our youth ministries really focusing on? What's the desired outcome of our time with kids? How much effort are we really putting into not only discipling, but also developing "Heathers" and "Aarons"?

"TO" OR "BY"

Millions of teenagers are apathetic about their faith, and their indifference greatly reveals itself each year when they graduate high school . . . *and exit their faith altogether*. It's a problem every youth worker in every denomination acknowledges.

When the Barna Group studied young college students who'd attended church as high school students, they found that these "twenty-somethings" were the most likely age group to drop church attendance. Once they left their homes, many of them left their faith, too.

The faith of many of our church kids could be described as nebulous and apathetic. This may sound critical, but sadly, our church kids don't look much different from kids who don't go to church at all. According to an in-depth poll by the Associated Press and MTV, 68 percent of American teenagers agreed with the following statement: "I follow my own religious and spiritual beliefs, but I think that other religious beliefs could be true as well." (*http://surveys.ap.org/data/KnowledgeNetworks/2007-08-20%20AP-MTV%20Youth%20 Happiness.pdf*) That might be expected from the pluralistic society we live in today, but when further research on the same subject was conducted by the Barna Group, it found that 61 percent of "Christian" teenagers believed if "a person is generally good or does enough good things for others during their life, they'll earn a place in Heaven." (*http://www.barna. org/barna-update/article/5-barna-update/137-religious-beliefs-remain-constant-but-subgroups-*

are-quite-different) That whopping 7 percent disparity clearly shows that many teenagers who go to church have a flawed faith.

In the last decade, I've seen the trend of youth workers who've tried to change this phenomenon with new curriculum and better teaching. But can a new Bible study do the trick?

Could it be that today's youth ministries are too focused on offering ministry TO teenagers instead of developing ministry BY teenagers? Maybe our "entertain me" programming mind-set has lowered the bar for many teens. Come, laugh, sing, listen, pray, exit.

What if we raise our expectations just a little?

Jim Burns, in his classic book *The Youth Builder*, forces us to ask a poignant question: "Are we creating spectators of the kingdom or participators and servants for the kingdom?" (*The Youth Builder*, 2001, Gospel Light, page 136)

What would happen if we gave teenagers opportunities to serve and use their gifts in ministry prior to high school graduation? What if we pour into these young leaders, disciple them, and do ministry alongside of them instead of for them? What if we ease back on our ministry *to* teenagers, supplementing it with more ministry *by* teenagers?

What if we ease back on our ministry *to* teenagers, supplementing it with more ministry *by* teenagers?

Perhaps then when these kids are out on their own and forced to take full ownership of their faith development, they'll have a strong foundation from which to start.

Like parents, our job as youth workers might just be to move kids from a position of dependence on *us* to dependence on *Jesus*.

This discipleship of our young leaders is a process; it's not instantaneous. Consider the time Jesus spent developing his disciples. He poured into them for three years, ministering alongside of them and giving them opportunities to develop their gifts and eventually take leadership roles. Upon first reading the Gospels, I had my doubts that these guys would amount to anything. On the day of the crucifixion, most of them abandoned Jesus altogether. But 11 of them went on to start spreading the good news about Jesus, the groundwork for what became "the Way" (Acts 9:2) and eventually the explosion of Christianity.

What do you think would happen if in the next few years you poured into a handful of teenagers who will, in turn, pour into others? What would happen to your ministry? More importantly, how would it help forge the faith of these kids and prepare them for life after high school?

Think of Aaron and Heather from the beginning of this chapter. If the youth pastor needed someone to lead the youth group, he called Aaron! Aaron not only led Bible studies and mission teams, but he also resolved to be a light on his campus when he was "out on his own" at school every day. When Aaron leaves high school, God will continue to use him this way. Aaron's already decided to own his faith, use his gifts, and serve.

As a middle schooler, Heather not only helped a bunch of her friends accept Jesus, but she also connected them to God's people at her church. When Heather went off to college, nothing changed. Heather continued to minister to others. I (Jonathan) know because I later invited her to be part of my youth ministry staff, where for several years she again led numerous young girls to Jesus, discipling them and connecting them to God's family.

Aaron and Heather didn't just receive ministry—they did ministry.

Aaron and Heather didn't just receive ministry—they did ministry.

And it didn't happen by accident or by playing dodgeball. Caring adults loved these two kids, discipled them, and gave them opportunities to serve and live out their faith. Soon they grabbed the baton, made their faith their own, and then loved and discipled others along the way.

How many "Aarons" and "Heathers" are you building right now?

If you're reading this book, then you're most likely in one of three places:

1. *You want to develop teen leaders but don't know how.* For right now that's okay; your reading this book reveals that you care about helping kids grow spiritually and you have a desire to see them use their gifts. Don't worry—we'll outline a step-by-step guide of exactly what you need to do to build teenage leadership ministry from scratch.

2. *You're trying to build a teenage leadership ministry but are running into opposition(s).* All sorts of problems can arise when you start pursuing the idea of mobilizing and equipping teams of kids to impact their communities for Jesus. We'll teach you how to generate momentum and build and maintain a team that works together, as well as sidestep any pitfalls that would stifle an enduring teenage leadership program.

3. *You've already built a teen leadership ministry, but you want a few ideas to bolster it.* You already have a few "Aarons" and "Heathers," but you want to develop even

more teen leaders. Maybe you're looking for a way to garner increased results from your existing teams. Regardless, you'll find tons of ready-made resources, proven strategies, and ideas sprinkled throughout this book that you can immediately implement.

So where do we begin?

Good question. Perhaps we should start by defining teenage leadership and taking a glimpse at what it could look like in your ministry.

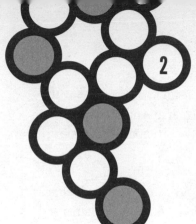

DEFINING TEENAGE LEADERSHIP

DEVELOPING TEENAGE LEADERSHIP IN YOUR MINISTRY

The term *teenage leadership* is used in a variety of circles. And the development of teen leaders in one church might look drastically different than a teenage leadership program at another church right down the street.

Is there only one proper way to develop teen leaders?

In the last chapter, we looked at a couple of examples of kids doing ministry, and we witnessed how exciting it is when teenagers use their gifts to make an eternal difference for the kingdom. Is that what we're referring to as teenage leadership?

Let's take a moment and put some nomenclature to this thing—when kids grow in their faith to the point that they want to use their God-given abilities to make an eternal difference. What do we call that?

Let's define some of these terms and then take a brief glimpse at the necessary process for implementing this into our ministries.

IS IT SERVING OR LEADING?

Serving . . . Leading . . .

Is there really a difference? It's an important question to address before we embark to develop a team of teenagers ready to do ministry.

David and I facilitated a fishbowl discussion about teen leadership at the Youth Specialties National Youth Workers Convention. I started by asking, "How much of our ministry should be run by teenagers?"

The youth leaders immediately suggested some percentages: "80 percent"; "No, 90 percent." It was really amazing to see the majority of these adult leaders excited about the concept of ministry *by* teenagers instead of just ministry *to* teenagers. And most seemed convinced that we don't need spectators in the kingdom; we need participants in and servants for the kingdom.

Isn't it nice when everyone agrees? (It didn't last long.)

The disagreement was about what to call ministry by teenagers. Was it *serving* or *leading*?

Some of the youth workers boldly stated, "All of our kids should be *leading*." Others used the word *serving*: "I try to give all my teenagers opportunities to serve."

We were so pleased with everyone's agreement about the importance of ministry *by* teenagers that we hesitated to start an argument about the finer semantics. But certain youth workers were interchanging the two words as if they were synonymous: "I give all my kids opportunities to *lead*." "We should always try to provide opportunities for all our kids to *serve*."

One youth worker even suggested, "All kids are leaders in their own way."

At this point I had to chime in. "I really don't agree with that statement." I wasn't comfortable with the free interchange of these two words. Then I simply asked, "Is there a difference between *serving* and *leading*?"

The discussion that followed was fascinating . . . *and frustrating*.

Most seemed to agree that all kids should be given the opportunity to serve. But they were divided about exactly how many kids should be leaders. Some said all kids are leaders. Others said only those who hold themselves to a biblical standard could be considered leaders.

Several youth workers shared personal stories: "What about a kid of mine who's addicted to pot? Should I not let him play on the worship team?"

I played the devil's advocate. "Well, the vocalist is a gossip. Should she be allowed to sing on the worship team?"

None of these are easy questions to answer. So let's start where most of us would agree: All of our kids should be given opportunities to serve.

I don't believe many youth workers would argue with that principle because service opportunities are usually growth opportunities. I probably wouldn't rob anyone of the chance to humbly serve someone else. When I worked with Youth for Christ/Campus Life, I used to take vanloads of unbelievers down to the local Salvation Army to serve the less fortunate. This was a great experience for these kids to get their hands dirty and care for the needy.

Yet, as much as I love feeding the homeless, washing feet, and doing service projects—none of these activities makes me a leader.

This book is about developing kids on a leadership team who will use their God-given abilities to make an impact for the kingdom. These "teen leaders" will get their hands dirty by serving, but serving doesn't make them leaders.

Here's an important principle to keep in mind: Every leader should serve, but not everyone who serves can lead.

Every leader should serve, but not everyone who serves can lead.

So who *can* be a teen leader?

SIDESWIPED BY SEMANTICS

Let's take a quick moment not only to clarify our definition of *teen leader*, but also to explain the need for our definition since it's the nomenclature we'll be using for the rest of the book.

In the business world, the word *leader* is used very differently than it is in the youth ministry world. Businesses are much more restrictive about who's labeled a leader, as they see leaders as being visionaries who mobilize other people to follow their vision. While they're pretty stingy with the "leader" title, we in youth ministry tend to label anybody who volunteers once a week—or even once a month—a leader. In the business world, the leader casts the vision and makes it happen. In youth ministry the kid who helps run the soundboard is called a leader.

The business world places all sorts of prerequisites and expectations on those it entrusts with the title of leader. Our youth ministry world usually isn't that refined.

But let's not knock the business world. We might be just as picky if the situation were dire enough.

Think about it for a moment: If you're on a plane that goes down in the Rockies, you're going to want a true leader to take charge of the situation and organize a strategy for survival. Will you stay by the plane or venture off in search of safety? Should the group split up or stay together? What resource is most important to the team's survival, and how will it be attained?

Somebody has to make those kinds of decisions and then forge those decisions into a positive reality. That's what a leader does. In fact, *only* leaders can do that.

To be a true leader, a person must lead others.

Does this sound like a new definition of *leadership* to you? Maybe not. But let's be honest. For a number of years, well-intentioned youth ministry thinkers have called every kid who serves or volunteers a *leader*. Kids who show up early to help set up chairs for worship are counted as leaders. Those who gather before school to pass out free doughnuts in the name of Jesus are called leaders. While neither of these examples qualifies as true leadership, both illustrate extremely important sacrifices.

Ever since David and I have been in youth ministry, *teen leader* has meant "any Christian kid who wants to serve and use his gifts." If you pick up almost any book on teenage leadership, it includes descriptions of kids who want to make an impact by serving God using their gifts—even those kids who aren't leaders by almost any definition.

These semantics aren't limited to kids, either. Most churches use these same terms for adults. Years ago I was part of an adult Sunday school class that had a leadership team consisting of six couples from the class. Of the 12 people on the team, only about six or seven were true leaders. The rest were well-intentioned Christians who chose to serve because they loved God and wanted to use their gifts to make an impact for God. Yet whenever any of those 12 people stood up in our adult fellowship group to make an announcement, they were introduced as leaders.

I've never seen anyone object to this nomenclature. We've just accepted it without critically thinking about it. When one of those servants of God was introduced as a leader of the group, no one ever stood up and yelled, "I object! I'd never follow this person through the Rockies!"

But it was a fact. About five or six people on that team not only wouldn't *want* to lead anyone through the Rockies, but they also *couldn't*. They weren't genuine leaders. They were wonderful people who were using their gifts, making an impact, and doing ministry; however, they were naturally wired to follow others.

This doesn't mean we don't want these types of people on our teams—quite the contrary. There's nothing like working alongside other committed believers who are growing, discovering their gifts, and seeking to make an eternal impact for God's kingdom. It seems we just don't know what to call them!

That said, let's not remain caught up in a debate on semantics. After all, what we're talking about is ministry *by* teenagers. We're talking about developing a team of kids who want to use their God-given strengths and abilities to make an eternal impact. Call them what you will.

But almost every book sitting on the typical youth worker's shelf refers to this type of a team as "student leadership." And this group usually contains a small number of authentic leaders—those who are wired to lead, people you'd follow through the Rockies. So in all fairness, it's not bad to call this group a leadership team. The team, as a whole, usually casts direction and leadership for the ministry; but in most cases, it also includes Christian kids who aren't necessarily leaders but are looking to use their gifts in ministry.

Rather than go against almost everything that's in print today, throughout the rest of this book we're going to go ahead and use the term *teen leader* to identify those kids we want to develop for ministry. As we prepare teenagers for ministry and develop teams of kids to do ministry, we'll also get numerous opportunities to develop some true leaders within that team. But we believe you'll find it rewarding to develop all kinds of kids for ministry—leaders and non-leaders alike.

At this point many of you might be asking, "What standard should we hold for these youth who will sit on our leadership team?"

A BIBLICAL STANDARD

Again, *leadership* is a word used in numerous ways. We're not talking about leadership as our culture defines it. We're talking about being a spiritual leader.

If I'm on the soccer field with a bunch of friends from the neighborhood, and we need to choose a captain, I won't require biblical standards of that person. ("I elect Carlos as our team captain. After all, he's the husband of one wife. He's not given to tantrums . . . .")

But if we're talking about leadership roles in ministry, then I'd refer to biblical standards like the ones we see in 1 Timothy 3:

> Here is a trustworthy saying: If anyone sets his heart on being an overseer, he desires a noble task. Now the overseer must be above reproach, the husband of but one wife, temperate, self-controlled, respectable, hospitable, able to teach, not given to drunkenness, not violent but gentle, not quarrelsome, not a lover of money. He must manage his own family well and see that his children obey him with proper respect. (If anyone does not know how to manage his own family, how can he take care of God's church?) He must not be a recent convert, or he may become conceited and fall under the same judgment as the devil. He must also have a good reputation with outsiders, so that he will not fall into disgrace and into the devil's trap. (vv. 1–7 NIV)

Notice that this list doesn't say that the overseer has to be perfect. If God were looking for only perfect people, we wouldn't have any leaders. But if God allowed just anyone to lead, then we'd go nowhere.

Passages like the one above give us some guidelines for discerning what we're looking for in the person and character of the kids on our leadership team. It's up to you to decide how detailed you want be as you set a biblical standard for these teenagers. I've seen some youth workers make a list of the traits in that 1 Timothy passage—almost like a checklist. And I've seen others use different passages altogether.

I like what Doug Fields did with his Saddleback youth years ago. Prior to the beginning of his teenage leadership program, he had his "core" kids come up with a portrait and profile of someone they respected as a teen leader based on biblical imperatives. This drove the kids to search Scriptures such as 1 Timothy 3 and other relevant passages. John 13 is another great passage to dissect—where Jesus modeled servant leadership by washing the disciples' feet. By doing this Doug's kids created their own standards based on relevant biblical truth.

Can you imagine the ownership teen leaders would feel while adhering to a biblical standard they'd penned for *themselves*? It's up to you how you want to communicate those biblical standards for the kids on your leadership team. The key is to do it.

And it goes without saying that the kids on our leadership team should be called to a higher standard. As you launch your teenage leadership program, it's okay to communicate that the leadership team isn't for everyone. Let kids know that you still love those who don't choose to meet these expectations and that God wants to continue working on them. Then back up those words with actions—loving all of your kids for who they are and spending time with them. If you have kids who are disappointed because they can't be on the leadership team, use that as an opportunity for discipleship. Let them know you'd love to meet with them and help them grow and develop their gifts—regardless of whether or not they're on the leadership team in the future.

We need to create an arena where *all* teens are valued—not just the ones on the leadership team. As a bonus, if you teach your leaders a Christlike model of servant leadership, then the other kids should feel even more valued as the teens on your leadership team make efforts to serve them, love them, and accept them all the more.

WHY THEY DO IT

As you can see, ministry *by* teenagers is different than just serving. Anyone can serve. Even celebrities will use their high-profile platforms to sway people to volunteer for a charity or feed the hungry.

While this book will encourage you to provide plenty of opportunities for *everyone* to serve, the focus is on preparing teenagers for ministry and developing teams of kids doing ministry. Doing ministry is much different than just serving. Kids who are doing ministry want to flesh out their relationships with Jesus by making a difference in the lives of those around them. They desperately want to make an impact for the kingdom of God. Stated another way, it's not so much *what* they do that sets them apart from those who serve, it's *why* they do it.

It's not so much *what* they do that sets them apart from those who serve, it's *why* they do it.

One teenager's act of "serving" could mean arranging chairs in order to get credited hours for community service, while another teen wants her friends to have places to sit when they come to worship God. Kids doing ministry understand the importance of sharing their faith, giving of themselves, leading sacrificial lives, and seeking to honor God in all they do.

They take their faith seriously. They live it out. They're focused on finding ways to bless others because they've been blessed. The Jesus who saved them has also called them to minister to others, and they wrestle with ways to do that best.

Imagine a whole team of these kids working together to accomplish this kind of ministry.

That's what this book is about—*ministry* by teenagers.

THE PROCESS OF DEVELOPING A TEENAGE LEADERSHIP TEAM

The question many of us might have at this point is, *What would this type of teenage leadership team actually look like in my ministry?* Is it something as casual as Jesus walking around and saying, "Come, follow me"? Or is it a regimented program with meetings?

Ministry by teenagers can have many faces. The last chapter of this book offers a snapshot of a number of real-life teen leadership programs. But deciding what you want teen leadership to look like in your own ministry is up to you. We've seen it function very casually in small ministries where pastors recognize potential in kids and simply ask them to step up and start serving and leading in some capacity. We've also seen structured programs with weekly meetings, service teams, and leadership retreats.

There isn't just one way to develop a teenage leadership team. In the remainder of this chapter, we'll show you an example of the steps you might take to develop a highly structured teenage leadership team. If your style of leadership requires less, then it will be easy for you to remove some of these steps. And we encourage you to pray through this entire process to see what God wants from you.

In addition, if you're without administrative strengths, we strongly encourage you to partner with someone who's very organized and can help you manage the teen leadership element in your ministry. Even the smallest and most casual teen leadership programs require some level of organization and management.

Let's take a look at this process where it begins—on our knees.

A FOUNDATION OF PRAYER

This principle is foundational, so you'll see us harp on this again. Don't start this venture on your own. Bathe it in prayer. Do you want your teenage leadership development to rest in human hands or in the hands of our mighty God?

As you recognize the need for growth and leadership in your ministry and consider how to carry out Jesus' commission to teach all nations about him—start out in prayer!

As you begin evaluating your ministry and taking the spiritual temperature of your kids—pray!

As you begin identifying and selecting teen leaders in your group—do so in prayer!

TAKE YOUR MINISTRY'S SPIRITUAL TEMPERATURE

Once you bathe this process in prayer, it's time to give your ministry a quick checkup. You'll want to evaluate the "spiritual temperature" of your ministry before you start building a structure of leadership.

In the next chapter, you'll go through the process of taking your ministry's temperature by taking a detailed inventory of the kids in your ministry. This step will help you determine not only the potential leaders, but also some areas of weakness in your ministry. Using that information will help you figure out exactly what you need in the way of service, ministry, and leadership. And that will help you . . .

LAY OUT THE SKELETAL STRUCTURE OF YOUR TEEN LEADERSHIP TEAM

Before you start recruiting kids for ministry and leadership, you need to have a rough idea of what your program will look like. Yes, I use the word *rough* purposely; it's important to stay flexible as you build this structure. New opportunities and ideas might require some restructuring. Regardless, you'll need a basic blueprint as you begin selecting kids.

If you've already been developing teen leaders, then you should have the momentum of structure in place. If building a teen leadership team is brand-new to you, then this chapter will help you with this important step.

Next, we've provided a checklist of steps to help you begin laying out what a teenage leadership program will look like in your ministry. Use the checklist as you go through this book.

In this part of the process, you'll start preparing the paperwork you need, documenting exactly how often your team will meet, how long the meetings will last, and what ministry teams you'll offer. These bare essentials are necessary before you invite teens to apply. Otherwise they won't know what's expected of them.

THE TEEN LEADERSHIP TEAM CHECKLIST: STEPS TO BUILDING YOUR STRUCTURE

Make certain you take the following steps to lay out the structure for your teen leadership team:

TAKE YOUR MINISTRY'S SPIRITUAL TEMPERATURE.

Take a detailed inventory of the kids in your ministry. Determine who potential leaders are, as well as some areas of weakness in your ministry. (Chapter 3 will help you with this.)

LAY OUT THE SKELETAL STRUCTURE OF YOUR TEEN LEADERSHIP TEAM.

- Create applications, commitment sheets, and any other forms. (We provide samples in chapter 4.)

- Document exactly how often your team will meet, when, and for how long. (We provide an example of this with our commitment sheet in chapter 4. And chapters 6, 7, and 8 will help you determine your training, team-building, and maintenance needs.)

- Will you host a teen leadership kickoff retreat? If so, when? Where? What will it cost? (We provide a complete teen leadership retreat agenda in the Appendix.)

- Decide what kinds of ministry teams you'll offer. (We provide a sample list in chapter 4.)

- Do you have an adult to mentor each ministry area?

IDENTIFY AND SELECT POTENTIAL TEEN LEADERS.

- Identify and select which kids you believe are ready to do ministry. (We talk about this process more thoroughly in chapter 4.)

- Announce your teen leadership program.

- Invite kids to apply.

- Interview kids.

- Partner kids with adult mentors.

CONTINUED ON NEXT PAGE

ASSIGN KIDS TO MINISTRY TEAMS.

Chapter 5 will assist you in helping your kids discover their ministries and leadership fits.

ORGANIZE YOUR TEEN LEADERSHIP TRAINING AND RETREAT.

Training is where the rubber meets the road in your teenage leadership development.

○ If you're planning a leadership retreat, what training topics will you cover? (See the complete leadership retreat agenda in the Appendix.)

○ What topics will you cover in your regular meetings? (See chapter 6.)

SCHEDULE REGULAR TEEN LEADERSHIP MEETINGS.

When you lay out your skeletal structure, you'll decide exactly how often your team will meet, when, and for how long.

○ Begin outlining and preparing the training topics you'll cover. (See chapter 6.)

○ What team-building activities will you do? (See chapter 7.)

○ How can you use these meetings to maintain the health of your team? (See chapter 8.)

IDENTIFY AND SELECT POTENTIAL TEEN LEADERS

At this point you'll want to identify and select the kids who you believe are ready to do ministry. We help you do this in chapter 4 by providing some ideas on how to notify your kids that you're building ministry leadership teams, as well as paperwork to help them apply for various positions. We'll give you a few tips for interviewing your incoming kids to ensure they're good fits for the vacant positions. Finally, we'll guide you through the process of choosing your final group of teens for ministry.

In that same chapter, we provide some applications and commitment sheets you can use as you identify and select potential teen leaders in your ministry. In our application we use some pretty broad biblical standards, such as, "lives a lifestyle befitting a role model and ambassador of Jesus." Then we spell out the exact commitment the kids would make, including some of the duties. Here's a couple of examples from the **My Commitment** sheet in chapter 4:

I'm committed to:

- regular church and youth group attendance;
- modeling a healthy commitment to my family;
- personal growth through Bible study and prayer;
- meeting weekly with an adult mentor (for Bible study, Bible verse memorization, and accountability);
- living a lifestyle befitting a role model and an ambassador of Jesus;
- being an example of proper behavior during worship services, programs, and activities;
- "being a light" on my campus, in my neighborhood, and in my home.

I'm excited about the following duties:

- Volunteering a minimum of two hours a week, in addition to regular youth programs and activities, in a specific ministry area (see **Ministry Area Choices** sheet);
- Attending teen leadership meetings on the first Sunday of each month;
- Attending the teen leadership development retreat on _____ (date);
- Completing regular reading assignments.

We'll go through these a bit more later on in the book. But you'll want to make sure to either copy our commitment and application forms or make up some of your own. These forms will help you clearly communicate your expectations to your kids.

ASSIGN KIDS TO MINISTRY TEAMS

After you identify and select all of the kids on your teen leadership team, it'll be time to assign them to ministry teams. (Chapter 5 will assist you in helping your kids discover their ministry and leadership fits.)

You can go about doing this in plenty of ways; we'll highlight a few of the most proven methods. You want your teen leaders to be blessings to others, so getting them into the correct roles will be important.

Again, we've tried to do all of the paperwork for you. We've got entire lists of ministry areas for you to consider throughout this part of the process. You'll want to use a list like this to help kids choose exactly where they want to serve.

It's nice to provide an adult helper or mentor for each ministry team. This will force you to examine how much adult help you need. We've seen teams that are 100-percent teen led, but we find it helpful when an adult with a heart for that ministry area serves on that particular team, too.

ORGANIZE YOUR TEEN LEADERSHIP TRAINING AND RETREAT

Once you've selected your kids and assigned them to ministry areas, you'll need to train them. One effective way to kick off your leadership team training is through a retreat—getting away together for 24 hours or a weekend. This time not only brings the team of kids together for the first time, but also trains them while clearly communicating the expectations of the ministry and leadership roles. Jonathan and I have used training retreats for years to get everyone geared up and on the same page to accomplish the youth ministry's goals for the year. Since we truly want to equip you with the resources to build a youth ministry leadership program from scratch, we'll provide you with training tips in chapter 6. And in the Appendix, we've spelled out an entire training retreat schematic to guide you through a whole weekend.

SCHEDULE REGULAR TEEN LEADERSHIP MEETINGS

Here's where you decide exactly when, where, how often, and for how long you'll meet with your kids in ministry and leadership. These ongoing meetings are crucial for your ministry and leadership teams' survival. During these meetings you can capitalize on the relationships you and your adult leaders have built with the kids. You can mentor and train them during these times. You can also focus on building unity on the teams through specific actions (something we'll address more in chapter 7).

This glimpse of developing a teenage leadership team is probably beginning to take form in your head and heart. We've described teen leadership long enough. Now let's go build it.

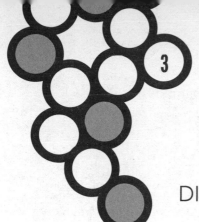

TAKING YOUR TEMPERATURE
DIAGNOSING YOUR NEED FOR MINISTRY BY TEENAGERS

"Okay, I agree it'd be exciting to see my kids leading and serving in our ministry and community."

That's what we hope you're thinking at this point. If you've just finished reading chapters 1 and 2, maybe we've not only sold you on the importance of developing teen leaders, but also provided a glimpse of what their leadership could look like in your ministry.

At this point, however, other questions might begin to surface:

- How do I know if I have any teenage leaders?
- If I have leaders, how do I spot them?
- How do I start developing teenage leaders?
- Why are those foaming soap dispensers so popular?

These questions are normal—at least the first three are. Some of us might wonder whether we actually have some potential teen leaders in our ministry just waiting for us to discover and train them. Who knows, maybe a kid we have contact with will be the next Charles Spurgeon. What an amazing opportunity!

Wait a minute!

What incredible *pressure*!

What if we mess up and he or she becomes the next Charles *Manson*?!

Don't worry. Seriously.

Don't let fear cause you to bail out of the process before it even begins. Developing teen leaders might appear a little cumbersome at first, but it's quite manageable when you break it down.

So let's take it one step at a time. We'll begin by looking at your ministry as a whole to determine your specific needs and then identify the potential to develop teen leaders. Trust me—the potential is there.

IS MY MINISTRY READY FOR THIS?

Some might be asking a huge question at this point: *As important as teenage leadership is, are my kids really ready for this?* There's only one way to find out.

Let's do a little exercise to help you take the temperature of your ministry. I believe you'll find that teenage leadership development is not only necessary, but also helpful in achieving the biblical goal of making disciples.

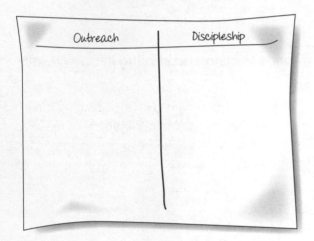

Take a sheet of paper and draw a line down the middle of it, making two columns. At the top of the left-hand column, write *Outreach*; at the top of the right-hand column, write *Discipleship*.

Everything we do in youth ministry can be divided into two general categories. In my last book, *Connect*, I (Jonathan) covered this extensively. (Don't worry if you already read that book, though; this won't just be review.) In this chapter we'll use this idea as a thermometer to assess our kids' need for leadership development, spiritual growth, or perhaps even salvation.

But before we do that, let's quickly define *outreach* and *discipleship* so we're crystal clear about the difference between the two. *Outreach* includes connecting with those who don't know Jesus and pointing to him through words and actions. *Discipleship* is helping believers to grow closer to Jesus and live more like him.

The kids we encounter will either be *outreach* kids (who don't know Jesus) or *discipleship* kids (who, at one time or another, made a decision to follow Jesus).

Some of you are already wondering if I'm oversimplifying things. *Do we assume all outreach kids are the same? Do all discipleship kids have the same attitudes and needs? Don't some youth show greater spiritual maturity than others?*

With these questions in mind, these two categories now appear pretty broad, don't they?

SIX TYPES OF KIDS

In our work with youth over the last two decades, we've noticed six types of kids who fit neatly into this table.

Go back to your piece of paper with the two columns. (Or just use the two-page table provided on pages 30–31.)

We're going to break down each column into three subcategories.

Now start with the left column—the Outreach side. There are three types of outreach kids: The No-Way Kid, the Not-Interested Kid, and the Checking-Things-Out Kid.

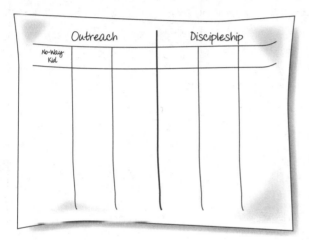

THE NO-WAY KID

The first kid we call the *No-Way Kid*. Write it as a subhead under the word *Outreach* on the far left side of the chart (as your first subcolumn). The No-Way Kid is resistant to church, Christians, and sometimes God. She's usually vocal about her feelings against Christianity, sometimes to the point of belligerence. I call her the No-Way Kid simply because she's quick to tell you there's "no way" you'll ever see her at church.

Have you met any of these No-Way Kids? If you've visited your local public school, you may have encountered them there. They aren't always rude or antagonistic, but they have no interest in church or spiritual matters.

If you work at a church, then chances are the No-Way Kids aren't in your youth group. The only way they'll attend, by definition, is if they're forced to go by Mom, Dad, or perhaps Grandma. After all, if it were up to them, there's no way you'd find them in church.

If you or your ministry *does* have contact with some No-Way Kids, write their names on your piece of paper in the No-Way Kid column now.

THE NOT-INTERESTED KID

The second outreach kid is the *Not-Interested Kid*. Go ahead and make that a subhead in the middle of the Outreach column. The Not-Interested Kid is probably the most common kid we'll find on a school campus. Typically he doesn't attend church. Yet it's not because he has anything against God or the Bible; he'd just rather be—anywhere else. He's simply *not interested*.

OUTREACH

NO-WAY KID	NOT-INTERESTED KID	CHECKING-THINGS-OUT KID

DISCIPLESHIP

STAGNANT KID	GROWING KID	LOOKING-FOR MINISTRY KID

Can you think of some Not-Interested Kids you've met? These kids most likely aren't attending youth group either, if it's up to them. They'd rather sleep in or watch football.

Both the No-Way and Not-Interested Kids aren't into coming to "our stuff." So if our outreach and evangelism efforts are limited to inviting kids to our stuff . . . then, sadly, we'll never reach these two types of kids.

Think for a moment about whether you know any Not-Interested Kids. If you or your ministry does have contact with some, then write their names in the appropriate column.

THE CHECKING-THINGS-OUT KID

The third type of outreach kid is the *Checking-Things-Out Kid*. Checking-Things-Out Kids are willing and open to engage in spiritual conversations and visit places where those conversations happen. They often recognize voids in their lives and are in search of answers. That's why they're open to *checking things out*.

These kids might actually come to church or Christian venues when invited. They're open to spiritual conversations. They're ripe to hear the gospel. Ministries that are perceptive to where these kids are at spiritually may even see them put their trust in Jesus. Sadly, many ministries miss opportunities to reach these kids because they blindly assume all kids at church are believers. If we miss these opportunities, Checking-Things-Out Kids simply "go with the flow," never hearing the gospel message.

Outreach			Discipleship		
No-Way Kid	Not-Interested Kid	Checking-Things-Out Kid			
Joe	Jill	Jed			
Bill	Dillon	Bo			
		Ali			

Do you have any contact with Checking-Things-Out Kids in your ministry? If so, write their names in the appropriate column.

• • •

Now let's look at the right-hand side of your paper—the Discipleship side. All of the kids we encounter on this side, by definition, have already put their trust in Jesus. And we don't determine on which side of this table our kids will fit. It's just a fact: Some kids have put their trust in Jesus, some haven't.

Furthermore, not all discipleship kids are perfect. Far from it. But at one time or another, they all have prayed and asked Jesus to forgive their sins and become Lord of their lives.

I see three types of discipleship kids, too.

THE STAGNANT KID

The first we call the *Stagnant Kid*. Stagnant Kids are those who made decisions to follow Jesus but never really grew in their faith. They're usually unplugged and can slip in and out of youth group without being noticed. They might attend fun events, but they usually aren't involved in Bible studies or small groups. They aren't connecting with other kids or growing in faith.

Their name says it all. They're stagnant. They need to get plugged into God's family, meet other believers, and grow in their faith. If you have some of these guys in your ministry, write their names on the left side of the Discipleship column.

If a Stagnant Kid gets connected and starts growing spiritually, then she becomes the next type of kid . . .

THE GROWING KID

The *Growing Kid* is exactly who we want our Outreach and Stagnant Kids to become: Plugged into God's people (the church) and growing in their relationships with Jesus. Growing Kids have put their trust in Jesus and are allowing him to transform their lives.

Do you have any Stagnant Kids or Growing Kids? Better yet, have you ever had the privilege of helping a Stagnant Kid become a Growing Kid? As youth workers we live for the moments when a kid's faith comes alive and real and we begin to see growth in his relationship with God.

If you have any Growing Kids, take a second and write down their names in the middle section of the Discipleship column. Include the names of any kids your ministry has contact with, even if it's not directly through the youth group.

THE LOOKING-FOR-MINISTRY KID

The sixth type of kid is the *Looking-for-Ministry Kid*. Looking-for-Ministry Kids are not only growing in their faith, but also looking for opportunities to minister in everyday situations. These are the leaders we're looking for.

Heather and Aaron (from chapter 1) are both Looking-for-Ministry Kids. Their faith has become so real to them that they can't help but share it with others. In addition, they're using their gifts to serve God.

But the fact that a particular kid serves others doesn't automatically make her a Looking-for-Ministry Kid. In fact, it's quite possible for No-Way Kids to be nice teens who care about others, participate in free car washes, and serve the homeless. The difference in the Looking-for-Ministry Kid is the Spirit-filled desire to make an impact for Jesus. Looking-for-Ministry Kids have a God's kingdom mind-set and are serving from an eternal perspective, not an earthly point of view.

We can help our Looking-for-Ministry Kids begin serving and leading in the areas of their God-given gifts. Kids with a God-given sense of compassion can use that gift to reach out to those in need. Kids with a God-given ability to teach can develop that gift, teaching others the truth from the Bible. It's amazing to see what happens once you help teens begin leading as God designed them to do.

If you have any of these kids, take a moment and write their names on the far right side of the Discipleship column on your piece of paper.

Outreach			Discipleship		
No-Way Kid	Not-Interested Kid	Checking-Things-Out Kid	Stagnant Kid	Growing Kid	Looking-for-Ministry Kid
Joe	Jill	Jed	Lindsey	AJ	Kim
Bill	Dillon	Bo	Ian	Bri	Mike
		Ali	Chris		

READING THE THERMOMETER

Okay, are you ready to take an honest look at your group? Let's finish what we've started on that piece of paper and fill in the names of all the teenagers we minister to.

Think of every kid you come in contact with, not just the ones in Sunday school or youth group. Fill in the name of every kid you've encountered in your ministry over the last six months or who your ministry influences in one way or another. If you have an open gym where kids come and play basketball, write down those names. If you go on campus to meet kids, write down the names of the kids you've been building relationships with recently. If you can't think of a kid's name, just write down a description (for example, "kid with glasses and blonde, spiky hair").

Figure out in which of the six subcolumns or categories each kid fits, and write his or her name there. This little exercise can be cumbersome. And forcing yourself to write these names might make you realize that you don't know the spiritual temperature of some of these kids. If you're having difficulty figuring out exactly who goes where, you might want to pick up a copy of *Connect* (Zondervan/Youth Specialties, 2009), which walks you through this process and devotes an entire chapter to ministering to each of the six types of kids (six chapters total).

For those of you who minister to only 10 or 12 kids, this exercise will be a snap. If you have 250 kids—come back to this chapter in two hours when you're done.

Are you finished?

Outreach			Discipleship		
No-Way Kid	Not-Interested Kid	Checking-Things-Out Kid	Stagnant Kid	Growing Kid	Looking-for-Ministry Kid
Joe	Jill	Jed	Lindsey	AJ	
Bill	Dillon	Bo			
		Ali			

Now let's take a peek and see exactly how ripe your group is for ministry by teenagers.

MACROANALYSIS

Let's look at the whole table from a macro perspective. (That's just a fancy way of saying from a bird's-eye view.) This will give you an overall, broad, inclusive look at the kids with whom you come in contact.

Which side of the table is fuller—Outreach or Discipleship?

Ask yourself, *Why?*

If the left side of the table contains more names, ask yourself what it would take to move more kids toward discipleship. Are you sharing Jesus' message frequently enough? Do you have others helping you reach out to all of these outreach kids? Do outreach kids have the opportunity to see Jesus in you and in your discipleship kids?

How would this table change if you had a few Looking-for-Ministry Kids who were helping you reach all of the kids on the Outreach side of the table?

If the left side of the page is full of names, it's pretty evident your ministry is not only ripe and ready for Jesus' gospel message, but it could also use the help of some Looking-for-Ministry Kids who are living out that message. Your program sure could benefit from ministry by teenagers.

Outreach			Discipleship		
No-Way Kid	Not-Interested Kid	Checking-Things-Out Kid	Stagnant Kid	Growing Kid	Looking-for-Ministry Kid
		Jed	Lindsey	AJ	Kim
			Ian	Bri	Mike
			Chris		

Conversely, if the right side of the table is fuller, ask yourself why you don't have contact with more outreach kids. Where are the outreach kids? Where do they hang out?

One answer is *on campus*. Most kids have to go to school by law. The high school and middle school campuses down the street from your church most likely contain the largest collection of outreach kids you'll find.

Now let me ask you another question: Who has the best opportunity and the open door to make an impact on campus?

The answer is your discipleship kids—or, more specifically, your Looking-for-Ministry Kids. That's right—teenager reaching teenager! Your right-column kids are not only right there on campus every day, but they're also *allowed* to talk about their faith. If we youth workers go on campus at most public schools across the country, we're *not* allowed to talk about our faith. Our right-column kids, however, have an open door to do so.

So if the right side of your table is fuller, then your ministry is ripe and ready to start developing Looking-for-Ministry Kids to reach out to your left-column (or outreach) kids. Your program is ready for ministry by teenagers.

MICROANALYSIS

Now let's take another look on a more micro level. In other words, look at the individual categories on each side of the table and see what these tell you about your ministry.

Start on the left side of the page—the Outreach side. How many No-Way Kids do you have contact with? How many Not-Interested Kids? Wouldn't it be cool if we had an open door to share Jesus with them? If you don't have contact with very many of these kids, then, again, ask yourself where these kids are. I think you'll find that your best resource to reach No-Way Kids and Not-Interested Kids is your Looking-for-Ministry Kids.

Now look at the right side of your piece of paper. Which category is the fullest?

If your Stagnant Kids column contains the most names, you're not alone. Your group is like the average youth group in America right now—a bunch of kids who made decisions for Christ at one time in their lives but aren't that committed. We talked about this depressing reality back in the first chapter. There's no doubt that it would be great if we could find a way to move these kids toward commitment and leadership. Consider how these kids would be affected if they were surrounded by Looking-for-Ministry Kids who were warm, welcoming, and excited about their faith. Developing Looking-for-Ministry Kids could create such an arena.

As you continue your microanalysis, some of you might notice that you have a lot of Growing Kids. These kids are plugged into church and growing in their faith. What would help these kids start moving toward Looking-for-Ministry—toward leadership?

What if they were encouraged to serve and start using their gifts? What if they were in an arena where discipleship was encouraged? Eventually, you'd probably see many of these kids become Looking-for-Ministry Kids. How can we move them toward the next column unless we provide a place for them? A teenage leadership venue might be just what you need.

Let me ask you: Are you providing opportunities for your "right-column" youth to develop their leadership skills and reach out to others?

Whatever the case, the solution that keeps rising to the top is *ministry by teenagers*.

The more I look at the needs of every kid from every category, the more I see the need to develop a team of Looking-for-Ministry Kids—kids using their gifts to make an eternal impact in the lives of their peers.

DISCOVERING DOORWAYS TO DISCIPLESHIP

I believe that you and your adult leaders will find this exercise helpful for taking the spiritual temperature of your ministry and even holding you accountable to spiritual growth as you see kids moving toward discipleship over time.

But how do we communicate the need for spiritual growth to one of our Stagnant Kids or Growing Kids? In other words, *we* might understand the need for spiritual growth, but how do we help our *kids* understand the need for spiritual growth? Do we show them the chart and tell them we believe they're stagnant?

Probably not a good idea!

But why not let them discover the truth for themselves?

A few years ago, I spoke to a group of teens about the parable of the sower in Matthew 13. I love this passage:

A farmer went out to sow his seed. As he was scattering the seed, some fell along the path, and the birds came and ate it up. Some fell on rocky places, where it did not have much soil. It sprang up quickly, because the soil was shallow. But when the sun came up, the plants were scorched, and they withered because they had no root. Other seed fell among thorns, which grew up and choked the plants. Still other seed fell on good soil, where it produced a crop—a hundred, sixty or thirty times what was sown. Whoever has ears, let them hear. (13:3–9)

As I told this story, describing the different soils and revealing the outcome for each seed, some kids weren't hearing the simple truth of it. I could see some of them deflecting the words as they left my mouth, not allowing them to penetrate. (*Hmmmm . . . "Whoever has ears, let them hear."*) Others were noticeably processing the story and thinking about the ramifications in their own lives . . . for about 15 minutes. As soon as the talk was done, many of those kids seemed to just shrug their shoulders as if to say, "Oh well. Back to the reality of my own little world."

But then there were kids who really absorbed the story. I could see them self-evaluating as the words touched their ears: "Which soil am I? Which soil does God want me to be?"

In the days that followed, I had the privilege of sitting down with some of those kids one-on-one. About 10 minutes into these conversations, I referred to the story and simply asked them, "Which soil do you think you are?"

These conversations were pivotal for some of the kids. Many of them were brutally honest with me. "I'm the thorny ground! I know I'm the thorny ground because every time I hear something in church, I know I need to do it. But then the next day I get with my friends, and the truth is choked out." I love these kinds of conversations—especially when teens are honest with themselves. And I find that most are pretty open and honest today. The question is whether they're willing to do anything about it.

At this point I like to use a conversational tool that my friend Greg taught me years ago. It's a layman's counseling method—one I've used hundreds of times in situations like the one I just described.

- Ask the kid, "Where are you now?"
- Then ask, "Where do you want to be?"
- Then offer, "How can I help you get from here to there?"

My friend Greg loved drawing on napkins. He'd draw one point on a napkin—Point A. "Where are you now?" Then he'd draw a second point on the other side of the napkin—Point B. "Where do you want to be?" Then he'd draw a line between the two with an arrow on one side. "How can I help you get from here to there—from Point A to Point B?"

That simple tool always sets the stage for discipleship and accountability. More importantly, it reveals doorways to spiritual growth.

This is of key importance. Don't miss this.

This practice helps kids discover doorways from which they can reach new levels of spiritual growth.

Isn't that what youth ministry is all about?

I've used the same method with outreach kids. *Where are you now?* Many teenagers have boldly told me, "I'm looking for something. I just don't know the answer yet." For me, that's an open door to share the gospel. Once, after I'd shared the gospel, a Not-Interested Kid named Ryan told me, "I know that's where I need to be, but I'm just not ready to make that commitment yet."

I totally respected Ryan's honesty, especially when compared with the numerous kids I've encountered who prayed words about accepting Jesus that they didn't mean. Besides, encountering a teen who's honest enough to admit he's not ready isn't the end of the road. After hearing Ryan's answer, I simply smiled and asked him, "Do you mind if I work on that?"

He laughed and said, "Go ahead. Give it your best shot!"

As you can see, we can even use this tool with outreach kids on occasion. Ryan heard the truth, and he knew it was the direction his life needed to go. Refusing to take that step, he nonetheless admitted his life was at Point A but needed to be at Point B. And when he told me I could "work on that," he gave me permission to help him get from "here to there"—Point A to Point B.

I'm constantly seeking opportunities to help kids discover pathways from Point A to Point B. Occasionally conversations about putting their trust in Jesus will happen with the three types of outreach kids. But most of the time, this is a tool I use when I'm talking with the three types of discipleship kids—helping them discover pathways from *where they are now* to a new level of spiritual growth.

What are some pathways to spiritual growth that you've witnessed in your ministry?

Do your kids want to get from Point A to Point B?

Have your Growing Kids ever considered that God wants to transform them into Looking-for-Ministry Kids? Do you know how to get them from here to there?

A teenage leadership program is a perfect tool to help you do that.

TEENAGE LEADERSHIP—A DOORWAY TO SPIRITUAL GROWTH

Imagine if spiritual transformation was *not* a priority in your ministry and doorways to spiritual growth were slammed shut. Imagine if your Stagnant Kids and Growing Kids were *not* discipled, encouraged, or held accountable. What if they were never given opportunities to serve or experience God working through them?

Not a pretty picture.

Now imagine if your Stagnant Kids and Growing Kids were discipled, encouraged, and held accountable by other believers. What if these kids were given opportunities to serve, see their own potential, and use their God-given gifts to make an impact for God's kingdom?

Of course, we'd all opt for kids who are growing, being discipled, and using their God-given strengths to make an eternal impact.

It's fun to see how excited kids can get about doing ministry. You might be surprised to see how many of them get excited when they hear they're gifted and God wants to use them for ministry.

Give it a try.

If you think about it, you have the opportunity to raise or lower the bar. You can help kids discover pathways from where they are now to new levels of spiritual growth . . . or you can let them stay where they are.

A teen leadership program might be just what you're looking for.

Enough! I'm convinced!

The stage is set, and you're ready for the meat and potatoes of developing a teenage leadership team. It's time to begin identifying and selecting your leaders.

RECONNAISSANCE
IDENTIFYING AND SELECTING TEENAGE LEADERS

You're about to enter fresh terrain—developing teen leaders in your ministry. Every new ministry year brings new kids with different gifts and a variety of potential. It doesn't matter how many times you've done this before. Each year presents uncharted territory with a new group of personalities.

It's time for a little reconnaissance.

Teenage leaders aren't going to start dropping from the trees. You have a key role to play—observing, identifying, and inviting teens to consider being used by God to do ministry.

It's sad but true. So let's go ahead and face facts: Not every kid we encounter is ready to do ministry. Thus, our first task in developing a teenage leadership team is to identify youth who are fit for the task. Although this is a big job, we can take a lesson from Jesus on how to do it.

IDENTIFYING TEENAGE LEADERS

Basically, Jesus had three kinds of people within his ministry that he could choose as leaders. There were the "multitudes," the "followers," and the "disciples."

MULTITUDES

When Jesus met people's needs, word got out. Usually the result was a huge crowd, such as in the feeding of the 5,000: "When the apostles returned, they reported to Jesus what they had done. Then he took them with him and they withdrew by themselves to a town called Bethsaida, but the crowds learned about it and followed him. He welcomed them and spoke to them about the kingdom of God, and healed those who needed healing" (Luke 9:10–11).

It seems this wasn't a rare occurrence. People often followed Jesus . . . even when he tried to slip off by himself (as in John 6:22–25).

The multitudes that followed Jesus consisted of interesting people. Some were there because of his teaching or healing. Some were there for a free meal, and some were even there to spy on him or try to catch him breaking the religious law of the day.

In our ministry we probably have crowds that are similar to Jesus' multitudes. True, they may not number in the thousands like Christ's, but we have youth who come to our ministries for many different reasons—some good and some not so good.

The kids listed on the left side of our Six Types of Kids chart would fit into this "multitudes" category. Jesus set an example of ministering to those "on the outreach side of the table," by going to where they were, feeding them, healing them, and preaching the good news to them. Sometimes he taught in the local synagogues; other times he taught in remote locations where the people had gathered.

Some of our Stagnant Kids might also be in this multitudes group. Even though they once made a decision to follow Jesus, they aren't plugged into a church or growing in their faith. These kids need our love and attention. We need to do everything we can to help them grow and get plugged into God's people. But until they're ready to take those steps, they choose to reside with the rest of the multitudes, living for themselves.

Even though the "multitudes" group is the largest, it's probably not the group from which we'll pull many teen leaders.

FOLLOWERS

Jesus also had a group that we'll call his "followers." These folks loved him and believed in him; and unlike the multitudes, they were willing to follow him wherever he went (hence their title). See Luke 8:1–3.

> After this, Jesus traveled about from one town and village to another, proclaiming the good news of the kingdom of God. The Twelve were with him, and also some women who had been cured of evil spirits and diseases: Mary (called Magdalene) from whom seven demons had come out; Joanna the wife of Chuza, the manager of Herod's household; Susanna; and many others . . . .

Oftentimes we forget that Jesus had more helpers than just the 12 disciples. In the Gospels we discover there were women and former blind men in this group. Even former dead people were Jesus' followers!

We have kids in our youth ministry who are like the folks in this group—minus the formerly dead people. (Or are your teens really *that* lazy?) They have an interest in growing their faith, and they're willing to order their lives accordingly.

Our Growing Kids are exactly like this group. In the last chapter we learned that Growing Kids are plugged into God's people (the church) and growing in their relationships with Jesus. Like Jesus' followers, Growing Kids have put their trust in Jesus and are allowing him to transform their lives one day at a time.

Some of our Stagnant Kids might actually move into this group of followers. One might argue that as soon as a Stagnant Kid starts growing and getting plugged in, she transforms into a Growing Kid. I agree. But we must realize that these lines are blurry. Our goal with all of these kids is to help them grow spiritually, thereby moving them over to the right side of our table. But this process takes time. If a Stagnant Kid responds to our love and attention, she might start to grow and get plugged into God's people. Who knows the exact moment she crosses over from Stagnant to Growing? And who cares—just as long as she does! The important thing is that we're always discovering doorways to move teens toward spiritual growth.

Potential teen leaders definitely exist in the followers group.

DISCIPLES

Finally, Jesus had the Twelve. This was the group of hard-core men who made continual sacrifices to be with Jesus, aid him in ministry, and carry on in his absence. He recognized these 12 guys to be so important to his work that he called them to join him in his ministry on a day-to-day basis. They're listed in Luke 6:12–16.

> One of those days Jesus went out to a mountainside to pray, and spent the night praying to God. When morning came, he called his disciples to him and chose twelve of them, whom he also designated apostles: Simon (whom he named Peter), his brother Andrew, James, John, Philip, Bartholomew, Matthew, Thomas, James son of Alphaeus, Simon who was called the Zealot, Judas son of James, and Judas Iscariot, who became a traitor.

We have teens in our ministry who are much like Jesus' Twelve. These kids might be the ones who hang around us all the time or are already doing something in our ministry—and maybe they show a desire to serve and lead even more. In the last chapter, we labeled these guys Looking-for-Ministry Kids. They're not only growing in their faith daily, but they're also looking for opportunities to minister in everyday situations. Looking-for-Ministry Kids are our teenage leaders, no question.

By the way, don't make the mistake of thinking that the term *teenage leader* implies someone who is outgoing or extroverted. Potential teen leaders might also be quiet kids who can use their gifts in behind-the-scenes roles. Introverted or extroverted, these kids are ready for God to use them to reach and serve others.

Teen leaders are definitely in the "disciples" group. We should be able to recruit most, if not all, of these teenagers for our leadership team.

Exercise

Go back to the Six Types of Kids chart that you filled out (in the previous chapter) while taking the "spiritual temperature" of your ministry. As we just saw, the people Jesus encountered would probably fit into this table quite neatly. So let's look at this table again—more specifically at the names you wrote in the rightmost two columns on the Discipleship side of the table.

If you want, you can write *Followers* near the heading of the Growing Kids column and *Disciples* near the heading of the Looking-for-Ministry Kids column.

Look at the names of the kids whom you believe fit in the "followers" or "disciples" categories. You'll personally want to invite these kids to be a part of the teen leadership team.

Outreach			Discipleship		
No-Way Kid	Not-Interested Kid	Checking-Things-Out Kid	Stagnant Kid	Growing Kid (Followers)	Looking-for-Ministry Kid (Disciples)
		Jed	Lindsey	AJ	Kim
			Ian	Bri	Mike
			Chris		

SELECTING LEADERS

Knowing where to look and what to look for is only the first step in the process of identifying potential teen leaders. We still have to *choose* them.

We're not qualified to choose leaders as Jesus did. If we're honest, we'd probably tend to make the same mistake that Samuel did thousands of years ago when he was tasked with choosing a king for Israel. Samuel wasn't looking for the same kind of person God was seeking. So God had to remind Samuel of this truth: "The Lord does not look at the things human beings look at. People look at the outward appearance, but the Lord looks at the heart" (1 Samuel 16:7).

Jesus knows people's hearts; we don't. Therefore, we need some help when it comes to making a final decision on who becomes a teen leader. An application process will provide that necessary help.

GET THE WORD OUT

Begin by announcing the leadership opportunities and providing some basic information about the possibility of serving as a teen leader. This publicity can be promoted in numerous formats. We've seen teen leadership teams promoted through announcements, fliers, webpages, and even videos and skits.

The best way we like to get the word out is to teach about it and encourage kids to discover pathways to spiritual growth. What better way to address teen leadership opportunities than to speak to their hearts about the issue?

This can be as simple as the example from the last chapter—teaching on the parable of the sower. Of course, this will be most effective when adult leaders *personally* follow up the teaching with one-on-one conversations and ask kids which type of soil they are (both where they are now and where they'd like to be).

Spend some time and energy getting the word out about the opportunity to serve as a teen leader. Don't rob the kids of the opportunity by announcing it just once. "Leadership applications are at the back of the room. They're due next Tuesday." (*We heard this announced right between the dodgeball tournament announcement and the skit about winter camp. Hmmmm . . . I wonder why no one picked up an application?*)

INVITE TEENAGERS TO APPLY

In addition to advertising the teen leadership opportunities to the masses, we also need to personally invite the kids we see as potential leaders. We can't stress this enough! Often youth workers believe that postcards, fliers, and generic announcements will suffice. Don't make that crucial mistake when it comes to building your teen leadership team.

Make sure you *personally invite* the kids whom you believe would make great leaders. The reason is simple: Some kids won't apply if they're not personally asked. Don't accidentally skip over the teenagers who may not believe they're "good enough" to lead. Your invitation might mean the world to them.

But be careful: We aren't inviting kids to become teen leaders—we're inviting them to *apply*. This might be as simple as walking up to one of your mature kids after a Bible study and saying, "Morgan, you've been really growing a lot in this past year. You should apply to be on the teen leadership team. I think you have the potential to be a great leader." Then if it doesn't work out with a particular kid, for whatever reason, you haven't overcommitted yourself to him.

I see the "getting the word out" stage as mere groundwork. Personal invitations are the beginning of finding teen leaders.

APPLICATION PROCESS

We've been referring to teen leader applications; so let's take a closer look at the application process. We've included three separate documents in this book:

1. The first is a simple **Teenage Leadership Team Application** that includes a **My Commitment** form. This application collects simple contact information, but it also asks a kid to describe his spiritual life. Its main job is to let us know if a particular kid is interested in ministry leadership. The **My Commitment** part of the application is a lot like a job description in that it lists the commitments all teen leaders will be responsible for keeping. Each leader is required to sign this commitment.

2. Next is the **Ministry Area Choices** page. This is a detailed list of the ways kids can lead in youth ministry. One place on this form invites kids to "write in" a position that isn't listed. If they want to bring something totally new to the ministry, this spot will give them an opportunity to describe it. (We'll be covering ministry areas extensively in chapter 5.)

3. Finally, there's a **Will You Be My Mentor?** form. It outlines the mandatory partnership that every teen leader must have with an adult leader for one-on-one personal development. Even the greatest, strongest, and brightest teenagers need a godly influence on their lives. Using this tool helps give teens that influence.

Let's walk through each of these forms, beginning on the next page.

TEENAGE LEADERSHIP TEAM APPLICATION

BASIC INFORMATION

Name: _____

Address. _____

Phone(s): _____ Email: _____

Parents'/Guardians' Name(s): _____

Grade: _____ Gender: (circle one) Male   Female

School: _____

JUST FOR KICKS

Favorite thing to do for fun: _____

Favorite type of music: _____

Favorite movie: _____

YOUR RELATIONSHIP WITH GOD

1. Please share when and how you became a Christian.

2. Please share what you're doing to continue growing in your faith in Jesus.

CONTINUED ON NEXT PAGE

3. Why do you want to be on the teenage leadership team?

4. How would your non-church friends describe your relationship with God?

5. How would your church friends describe your relationship with God?

6. How would your family describe your relationship with God?

MY COMMITMENT

I have a personal relationship with Jesus Christ and live by faith, following his example and obeying his commands in the Bible.

I'M COMMITTED TO:

- regular church and youth group attendance;
- modeling a healthy commitment to my family;
- personal growth through Bible study and prayer;
- meeting weekly with an adult mentor (for Bible study, Bible verse memorization, and accountability);
- living a lifestyle befitting a role model and ambassador of Jesus;
- being an example of proper behavior during worship services, programs, and activities;
- "being a light" on my campus, in my neighborhood, and in my home.

I'M EXCITED ABOUT THE FOLLOWING DUTIES:

- Volunteering a minimum of two hours a week, in addition to regular youth programs and activities, in a specific ministry area (see **Ministry Area Choices** sheet);
- Attending teen leadership meetings on the first Sunday of each month;
- Attending the teen leadership development retreat on _____(date);
- Completing regular reading assignments.

TRAINING AND DEVELOPMENT DETAILS

Monthly Leadership Meetings
- Prayer time
- Teen-led Bible studies
- Discussion on assigned reading
- Ministry reports/decisions
- Training
- Working in ministry area teams

Leadership Retreat
- Worship/fellowship
- Team-building
- Training:
  Live like Jesus.
  Love others.
  Serve humbly.
  Discover/develop your spiritual gifts.

CONTINUED ON NEXT PAGE

CHOOSE A MINISTRY TEAM

Ministry Areas
- Evangelism Team

- Thursday Night Leadership Team

- Service Project Team

- Contact Team

- Tech Team

- Missions Team

- Special Events Team

- Teaching Team

- Drama Team

- Middle School Staff Team

- Administrative Team

Monthly Training Topics
- Leading a small group/Bible study

- Engaging in spiritual conversations

- Sharing your faith

- Programming with a purpose

I've read all of the above and accept the Leadership Team Commitment.

Youth Signature _____ Date_____

Parent Signature _____ Date _____

THE LEADERSHIP APPLICATION

The teenage leadership application isn't a simple name and address form. It also asks questions about the kid's relationship with God and asks her to speculate on what other people see in her.

These kinds of questions about faith and day-to-day actions are not only a great screening tool, but also a good discipleship tool.

I (Jonathan) once had a kid fill out the exact application provided in this book. When he got to question number two, he got stuck. I loved this kid's honesty. He came up to me and asked me, "What do you mean by 'grow' in your faith?"

Thirty seconds into this conversation, I realized this guy really had no idea what a relationship with God was all about. So I shared the gospel message with the kid. He prayed with me right there and put his trust in Jesus.

I told him I'd love for him to be a leader, but I thought he and I should go through a discipleship book first so he could learn a little more about what this relationship with God looked like. I discipled the kid for six weeks using a book that went through the foundations of the faith. Then he reapplied, filling out that application with a new confidence.

I've said it before, and I'll gladly repeat myself: This is one of the bonuses of a teen leadership program. It can open incredible doors to one-on-one discipleship! Create an arena where no kid is left behind. Some kids will become leaders. Some kids might apply and not be ready. Don't dismiss these kids. Use this as an excuse for you or one of your adult leaders to spend time with them and disciple them, too.

The leadership application is a great discussion starter, but most of all it helps us evaluate whether someone is ready to be on the leadership team.

This application packet also includes a **My Commitment** sheet for the teen to read and sign. This commitment sheet is like a job description, offering an overview of the program and stating the requirements and expectations of the leadership team.

Looking at the form we've provided in this book, you'll notice we lay out the exact commitments we require.

I am committed to:

- regular church and youth group attendance;
- modeling a healthy commitment to my family;
- personal growth through Bible study and prayer;
- meeting weekly with an adult mentor (for Bible study, Bible verse memorization, and accountability);
- living a lifestyle befitting a role model and ambassador of Jesus;

- being an example of proper behavior during worship services, programs, and activities;
- "being a light" on my campus, in my neighborhood, and in my home.

We also list some of the main duties.

- Volunteering a minimum of two hours a week, in addition to regular youth programs and activities, in a specific ministry area (see **Ministry Area Choices** sheet);
- Attending teen leadership meetings on the first Sunday of each month;
- Attending the teen leadership development retreat on _____ (date);
- Completing regular reading assignments;
- Washing the youth pastor's car. (*Okay, this one's optional. But you won't know until you ask, right?*)

We want to state these requirements and expectations *up front* so kids know what they're committing to. You'll also notice that we require a parent signature on the application. We want parents to know and agree with what their kids are committing to.

This application can help you select teens who want to make a difference and are willing to invest their time. Feel free to customize your application as needed. You may choose to be a little more flexible or a little more rigid.

MINISTRY AREA CHOICES

Our application lists a few of the ministry areas that kids can choose. To give youth a clear picture of some of the areas in which they can serve, it's nice to provide a **Ministry Area Choices** form.

We've provided a sample form for you, which lists a large number of ministry areas for which kids can apply themselves in a leadership program. Yes, our form provides almost too many teams. We just want you to see numerous examples of ministry areas. Most teenage leadership teams won't have this many areas for the simple reason of numbers. (Most of these teams would require several people. So unless you have at least 40 teen leaders, having as many teams as our list supposes is highly unlikely.)

Your form might look a lot different depending on your needs and opportunities, but this example should provide a good idea of what the form *could* be. One kid might help administer outreach programs, while another maintains the youth database. Creating a variety of ministry jobs or leadership roles might seem cumbersome to plan or maintain, but the reward is well worth it.

If you want to see brothers or sisters in Jesus blossom, find their gifts and enable them to use those gifts. There's no greater joy than God using you in the area of your gifting. We'll talk about gifting in greater detail in the next chapter because it's crucial to help kids discover their passion, gifts, and strengths so they can use those in your ministry.

MINISTRY AREA CHOICES

This form lists the various areas of leadership available to teenagers. Read over the list of possible positions you could fill in our youth ministry and check all that you're interested in. We'll help you determine a final fit later.

○ SERVICE PROJECT TEAM

Kids plan regular service opportunities where anyone in the youth ministry program can experience serving the needy.

Duties Include:

- Contacting service organizations
- Organizing service projects
- Communicating and advertising service opportunities

Skills Required:

- Organization
- A heart for service

○ TEACHING TEAM

Kids on this team will help lead Bible studies or small groups for other teenagers.

Duties Include:

- Preparing lessons
- Setting up meeting spaces
- Working closely with other group leaders
- Teaching or leading the small group

Skills Required:

- Listening skills
- Up-front leadership
- Teaching ability

CONTINUED ON NEXT PAGE

○ MISSIONS TEAM

Kids on this team will plan one annual mission trip, as well as a handful of short mission events.

Duties Include:

- Contacting mission organizations
- Organizing mission trips
- Communicating and advertising mission opportunities

Skills Required:

- Organization
- A heart for missions

○ DRAMA TEAM

This team will produce skits, dramas, and sketches for use in our youth ministry.

Duties Include:

- Finding or writing material for use
- Practicing the skits or dramas for youth ministry
- Working with the worship team to ensure the proper "fit" of the material

Skills Required:

- Up-front leadership
- Love of acting
- Artistic creativity

○ WORSHIP TEAM

Kids on this team may sing, play instruments, or help with sound for the worship band.

Duties Include:

- Finding or writing music
- Attending weekly practices
- Leading weekly worship sessions

Skills Required:

- Up-front leadership
- Vocal, instrumental, or technical sound ability

○ FOLLOW-UP TEAM

This team will contact new teenagers or new Christians each week (or as needed).

Duties Include:

- Maintaining correspondence (email, snail mail, texting)
- Making phone calls
- Using social networks
- Developing and managing a database of new teens
- Working closely with the evangelism team

Skills Required:

- Administrative skills
- Hospitality and friendliness
- Care and compassion

○ MIDDLE SCHOOL LEADERSHIP TEAM

Kids on this team will act as "interns" for the middle school ministry at the church.

Duties Include:

- Mentoring a middle schooler
- Attending middle school group on certain nights

Skills Required:

- Relational skills

○ TECH TEAM

This team will oversee sound, lights, and video for our youth ministry programs and productions.

Duties Include:

- Operating sound system for programs and practices
- Operating lighting system for programs and practices
- Shooting and editing video

Skills Required:

- Technological skills

CONTINUED ON NEXT PAGE

◯ OFFICE SUPPORT TEAM

Youth on this team will assist in the administration of the youth ministry.

Duties Include:

- Assisting regularly with office work
- Helping with phone calls
- Helping with mailers
- Helping with paperwork

Skills Required:

- Administration
- Organization
- Computer skills

◯ MARKETING TEAM

Youth on this team will design and produce paper and digital forms of advertising.

Duties Include:

- Developing strategies of publicity
- Designing fliers, newsletters, emails, etc.
- Distributing all forms of advertisement
- Working with schools to gain permission to market on campuses

Skills Required:

- Computer skills
- Administrative skills
- Organization
- Creativity

◯ EVANGELISM TEAM

The evangelism team is made up of kids who are constantly looking for ways to live the gospel in both words and actions.

Duties Include:

- Working to reach kids who don't go to church
- Planning events targeting those kids
- Organizing events to reach those kids

Skills Required:

- Organization
- Teamwork
- Compassion

◯ GREETER TEAM

This team will welcome all kids to youth ministry programs and events.

Duties Include:

- Attending all youth ministry functions
- Making ALL kids feel welcome
- Handling registration at the front door

Skills Required:

- Hospitality
- Friendliness
- Organization

◯ PRAYER TEAM

Youth on this team will provide frequent, confidential prayer for the ministry and kids in our programs.

Duties Include:

- Praying for teens and adults in our youth ministry
- Leading events or sessions of prayer for others
- Asking for prayers from youth
- Managing prayer request records

Skills Required:

- Compassion
- Passion for prayer
- Confidentiality

◯ FOOD/SNACK TEAM

This team will prepare and serve food and snacks to kids and adults at our youth ministry.

Duties Include:

- Cooking, making, or preparing food
- Serving food
- Cleaning up after meals

Skills Required:

- Culinary skills
- Organization

CONTINUED ON NEXT PAGE

○ GAME TEAM

Kids on this team will develop and lead fun activities for the group.

Duties Include:

- Finding or designing fun, cool, safe games
- Leading games for the group
- Collecting various props (as needed)

Skills Required:

- Up-front leadership

○ _____ TEAM

In the space provided, name a team that you believe our youth ministry should have—and one that you'd be willing to serve on. Then write a brief description of the necessary duties and skills below.

WILL YOU BE MY MENTOR?

I (Jonathan) have always required my teenage leaders to meet weekly with adult mentors. This is a great excuse to require something that I deem priority one in youth ministry.

I don't need to talk too much about this because I already wrote an entire book on the subject: *Connect*. In that book I not only provided research revealing the importance of adults mentoring teens one-on-one, but I also laid out a plan for how to connect with the six types of kids. I even dedicated an entire chapter to mentoring the Looking-for-Ministry Kid.

The **Will You Be My Mentor?** form (page 60) that we've provided in this book is just a document to help you connect your youth with adult mentors.

Think about what an amazing opportunity this is. Our teen leadership team can require kids to meet with adult mentors—a practice that might just turn out to be a life-changing experience for both teens and adults.

My home church is great at connecting mentors with teen leaders. All of our teenage leaders are required to meet with mentors at least once a week for prayer and encouragement. We have way more teen leaders than adult youth leaders, so kids have to find mentors beyond the youth room. Kids ask ushers, music ministers, and laypeople who aren't even connected to the youth ministry program to be their mentors. It's amazing to see adults from all corners of the congregation being used in mentorship roles.

Safety is always important, so these mentors have to fill out the mentor application form. I also recommend putting all mentors through a background check that includes fingerprinting. (I spend an entire chapter talking about these kinds of precautions in my *Connect* book.)

WILL YOU BE MY MENTOR?

As a teenage leader for _____ (church name), I need to meet weekly with a Christian adult mentor. I was wondering if you'd like to consider being my mentor. A mentor is a caring adult who's willing to meet with me weekly, talk about my highs and lows, and work through a book or discipleship guide with me. All discipleship materials will be provided.

Teenager's Name: _____

Please fill out this basic information sheet.

Mentor Name: _____

Address: _____

Phone: _____ Email: _____

Have you ever discipled or mentored someone before?   Yes   No   (circle one)

Please provide details about the experience.

If needed, would you be interested in meeting with two teenagers (in one meeting)? _____

When would you be available to meet? _____

1. Please share when and how you became a Christian.

2. Please share what you're doing to continue growing in your faith in Jesus.

INTERVIEWS

After kids turn in their applications, you'll need to perform a filtering process. We recommend you do this by first reviewing the applications with some of your adult leaders, and then setting up interviews with the kids.

Even though I like to involve several of my adult leaders in the selection process, I usually do the interviews alone or with just one other adult leader. Teens are nervous enough during these interviews; imagine having five adults sitting in the room as a kind of "parole board." I do my best to make these interviews as comfortable as possible for them.

The interviews will be the final screening. They're also good tools for hearing teens' hearts and listening for the ministry areas in which they might be interested in serving.

Realize that your kids will have jumped through a lot of hoops by this point. Kids who aren't ready for the leadership team probably will have eliminated themselves by this stage of the process. A good application will filter out a lot of the kids who shouldn't be applying. Some teens know, for example, that they don't meet the requirement of "living a lifestyle befitting a role model and ambassador of Jesus."

I once had a guy who showed great leadership skills. Other kids in the church loved him, he was popular on campus, and he was great up front. I would have loved to have had this kid on my teen leadership team. But he couldn't keep his temper in check or his mouth shut. It seemed as though there wasn't a youth event at which he *didn't* get in a fight, mouth off to one of my adult leaders, or just disrupt things in general. Bottom line: He didn't "live a lifestyle befitting a role model and ambassador of Jesus."

I hate turning away a teen who wants to be on the team. That's why I set up such a stringent application and interview process. Think about it: Almost any kid who fills out the application, gets a weekly mentor, and commits to the time commitment is basically in. But every once in a while, you'll interview a teen who shouldn't be on the team. Use this as an opportunity for discipleship. Talk with her about the problem and lay out a plan to work on it with an end goal of joining the team. This is one of those great counseling opportunities where if she recognizes herself at Point A but wants to go to Point B, you can help her get there. The teen leadership program might even be a goal for the future. This can work as an incredible motivation for life change in kids.

You'll also have kids whose applications are flawless and interview well . . . only to watch them break their commitments after weeks or even months of being on the leadership team. Kids like this need to be removed from leadership, but it must be done with the same love and care discussed earlier. We'll go into more detail about removing teens from leadership in chapter 9.

MEET THE PARENTS

Oftentimes you can include parents in the application process. You might consider making a meeting with the parents a required part of the interview process. As soon as kids are accepted, you'd simply schedule a meeting with their parents as the final step, going over the expectations and opening up the communication channels between all parties.

This isn't a staple of the application process by any means. Some ministries have great success with parents being involved in the interview process; others find that this step could keep some kids from applying. Sadly, some parents aren't supportive of their kids' church involvement. Thus, this step might become a roadblock for those kids.

Whatever you decide, make sure that—at a bare minimum—you keep the channels of communication open with the parents. If you decide not to include parents in the interview process, at least try to include a parent signature on the application form so parents are aware of their kid's commitment to the leadership team.

"CONGRATULATIONS—YOU'RE ON THE TEENAGE LEADERSHIP TEAM"

When the dust settles, you'll have a group of teens who've been prayerfully chosen to help you lead and grow your ministry. But first you'll need to help them find their fit.

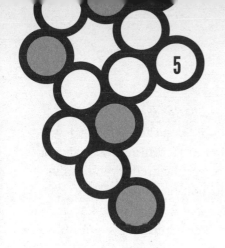

ROUND HOLE, ROUND PEG . . . SQUARE HOLE, SQUARE PEG . . .

HELPING TEENAGERS FIND THEIR LEADERSHIP FITS

Every teenager in your leadership program will have places or positions in which he thrives. And filling a certain role in the ministry will allow him to bless others radically. That's called a "leadership fit," and helping each teenager discern his leadership fit will be the next key move in developing a strong teen leadership program in your ministry.

When we learned about shapes when we were kids, we did so by matching pegs with their corresponding holes. We soon realized—at least *most* of us did—that round holes require round pegs, square holes require square pegs, and so on. A triangle peg won't fit into the oval hole no matter how hard we force it. The same rule applies to leadership fits.

If we get it right, we can understand why Jesus said his church would stand up against the attacks of hell. But if we get it wrong—well, *it just feels like hell*.

Think about how silly the following "fits" would be.

You're invited onto the set of an upcoming blockbuster film to see the operation in action, meet the cast, and witness how the magic is made. For several hours you quietly sit in a folding chair next to the director, collect several autographs from some of your favorite celebrities, and try to figure out how you can "acquire" one of the red-hot convertibles that the stunt drivers are using. That's when you notice that one of the stunt drivers is none other than famed director and producer Steven Spielberg. Instead of using his years of experience behind the camera or tapping into his expertise in finding the perfect shot, he's dangling from aircraft cable, leaping from fast-moving UFOs, and dodging the mutant chicken's attacks.

I know what you're thinking: *What kind of movie is that?*

What you *should* be thinking is, *What a terrible fit for someone like Spielberg!*

Or maybe you walk into the arena to watch LeBron James shoot hoops and school a few lesser players. You look out over the court a few times, but you can't find him. You glance over at the bench, but he's not there either. Then, on your way out of the arena, you finally spot LeBron behind the counter of one of the concession stands, boiling hot dogs.

They're using one of the most talented players in the NBA as a hot-dog cooker? you ask yourself incredulously. LeBron was created to slam-dunk and shoot fades, but they've got him cooking stadium dogs. That's as ridiculous as Michael Jordan playing baseball. Oh, wait a second . . . .

Talk about bad fits. Can you imagine the world of film without Spielberg? No *E.T.* or *Jaws.* What if LeBron was never again allowed onto the basketball court and just labored behind the concession counter instead?

In other words, we'd feel a few distinct voids in our world if these scenarios had ever played out.

In a similar way, if your kids aren't serving in their proper leadership fits, you'll feel distinct voids within the kingdom of God as well.

FINDING THE FIT

By now I believe you can see how important it is to help your teenagers discover their leadership fits. But a few questions remain:

- Do I let them choose what they want to do and hope they get it right?
- Should I go with a trial-and-error approach until I find a position suitable for each kid?
- Is it unspiritual of me to whip out a fortune-telling crystal ball or play "Eeny, meeny, miney, mo"?

Ministry leaders have tried many ways to help teens find their leadership fits—some better than others. But here are a few proven strategies that'll help you guide your kids into their leadership fits.

PRAYER

We're not talking about prayer again simply because we want to cover the spiritual bases. We're including it because it's worked for thousands of years! Whenever biblical leaders needed to appoint others, they usually did so after prayer. Though the Bible is filled with these instances, here are a few quick examples.

When Abraham's servant was charged with finding a wife for Isaac, a role that necessitated much responsibility in those days, the servant began his search in prayer.

Then the servant left, taking with him ten of his master's camels loaded with all kinds of good things from his master. He set out for Aram Naharaim and made his way to the town of Nahor. He had the camels kneel down near the well outside the town; it was toward evening, the time the women go out to draw water.

Then he prayed, "LORD, God of my master Abraham, make me successful today, and show kindness to my master Abraham. See, I am standing beside this spring, and the daughters of the townspeople are coming out to draw water. May it be that when I say to a girl, 'Please let down your jar that I may have a drink,' and she says, 'Drink, and I'll water your camels too'—let her be the one you have chosen for your servant Isaac. By this I will know that you have shown kindness to my master."

Before he had finished praying, Rebekah came out with her jar on her shoulder. She was the daughter of Bethuel son of Milkah, who was the wife of Abraham's brother Nahor. The girl was very beautiful, a virgin; no man had ever slept with her. She went down to the spring, filled her jar and came up again.

The servant hurried to meet her and said, "Please give me a little water from your jar."

"Drink, my lord," she said, and quickly lowered the jar to her hands and gave him a drink.

After she had given him a drink, she said, "I'll draw water for your camels too, until they have had enough to drink." So she quickly emptied her jar into the trough, ran back to the well to draw more water, and drew enough for all his camels. Without saying a word, the man watched her closely to learn whether or not the LORD had made his journey successful.

When the camels had finished drinking, the man took out a gold nose ring weighing a beka and two gold bracelets weighing ten shekels. Then he asked, "Whose daughter are you? Please tell me, is there room in your father's house for us to spend the night?"

She answered him, "I am the daughter of Bethuel, the son that Milkah bore to Nahor." And she added, "We have plenty of straw and fodder, as well as room for you to spend the night."

Then the man bowed down and worshiped the LORD, saying, "Praise be to the LORD, the God of my master Abraham, who has not abandoned his kindness and faithfulness to my master. As for me, the LORD has led me on the journey to the house of my master's relatives." (Genesis 24:10–27)

The prophet and judge Samuel was tasked with finding another king for Israel after God rejected Saul. Through ongoing conversations God led Samuel to young David. Samuel didn't revert to a self-help book such as *King-Anointing for Dummies*; he just bathed the process in prayer. (You can read about the details of that event in 1 Samuel 16.)

Even Jesus, the perfect Son of God, prayed before assigning leadership fits. Luke 6:12–16 shows exactly how Jesus used prayer throughout his earthly ministry.

> One of those days Jesus went out to a mountainside to pray, and spent the night praying to God. When morning came, he called his disciples to him and chose twelve of them, whom he also designated apostles: Simon (whom he named Peter), his brother Andrew, James, John, Philip, Bartholomew, Matthew, Thomas, James son of Alphaeus, Simon who was called the Zealot, Judas son of James, and Judas Iscariot, who became a traitor.

Think about the significance of those leadership fits. These guys weren't going to be the "roadies" for Jesus' earthly ministry; after his ascension, they were going to plant churches, preach the gospel, and help write the New Testament so millions might read and believe. Even Jesus wanted God the Father to weigh in on his choices for leadership fits.

Finally, the early church followed Jesus' example and prayed. Prayer played a role in the selection of the men who were to oversee the daily distribution of food (see Acts 6) and also in the missionary journeys of Paul (then known as "Saul") and Barnabas (see Acts 13:1–3). And when those two great missionaries needed to appoint leaders in the churches they planted, guess what they did. That's right—they prayed. Check out Acts 14:21–23.

> They preached the gospel in that city and won a large number of disciples. Then they returned to Lystra, Iconium and Antioch, strengthening the disciples and encouraging them to remain true to the faith. "We must go through many hardships to enter the kingdom of God," they said. Paul and Barnabas appointed elders for them in each church and, with prayer and fasting, committed them to the Lord, in whom they had put their trust.

Too many biblical examples of the prayerful selection of leaders exist for us to overlook this practice. No matter how well you know the situation, God knows it better. No matter how well you understand the personalities involved, remember that God created those people. No matter how determined you are to see ministry happen, God is the One who gave the life of his Son to see it come to fruition.

Because of *God's* role in *your* ministry, you probably should ask God for (a lot of) help when it comes to making leadership fits. But talking to God about your ministry needs is only half the conversation you need to have. You still need to talk with your teens about their roles in ministry leadership.

DISCERNMENT THROUGH MENTORING RELATIONSHIPS

For ages God has used older, wiser, and more mature believers to guide younger and less mature ones. Moses did it for Joshua, Jesus did it for his disciples, and Paul did it for Timothy. The use of these mentoring relationships is as noticeable in Scripture as the practice of prayer mentioned above.

Think about it for a moment. God began a relationship with us through Jesus. We build relationships with others so we can share the relationship we have with Jesus in the hope that they'll also begin a relationship with him. Want to guess what the key is here?

Right—*relationships.*

Why not capitalize on the relationships you have with your kids and help them find their leadership fits? (And don't forget to have your adult volunteers help with this process as well!) A great way to do this is through one-on-one conversations that focus on specific facets of kids' lives.

HEART

Peyton couldn't see past the end of his walking stick because he'd been born legally blind. But his older brother, Drake, had 20/20 vision. Even though Drake was a popular high school football player, his first priority was always his middle school brother who loved *Star Wars* and insisted on quoting Yoda and Chewbacca in every conversation.

Drake watched out for his little brother and always had a mind for "What does Peyton need?" "Is Peyton all right?" and "What can I do to help Peyton fit in?" Since Drake literally grew up with a kid who had special needs, it showed in his life.

Drake naturally saw others through that same filter. Drake could walk up to me and say, "The girl by the Ping-Pong table looks like she's alone," or, "The guy in the red shirt needs someone to talk to." Drake didn't have ESP; he just paid attention to people's needs.

Looking after others was a part of Drake's DNA. It came to him as naturally as breathing.

So whenever I needed to make sure that everyone in the room felt welcomed and loved, I turned to Drake. When it came to taking care of people, Drake was my man. Every visitor to our ministry knew Drake. He made it a point to meet people *and* help meet their needs.

God had supernaturally used the environment that Drake grew up in with his younger brother, Peyton, to carefully craft a heart that beat for others. In our youth ministry, that heart advanced God's kingdom.

That's "heart." It's the stuff we do without even thinking about it. It's our natural (or supernatural) reaction to a situation that injects God's love into it. Most of your teenage leaders will show some evidence of this, but it's up to you and your adult leaders to help them use their hearts to lead others.

Keep your eyes open and "heart" will be easy to spot. What heart do you see emanating from the lives of your kids?

Even though your own power of observation will be the best tool for spotting heart, you can also get a glimpse of your kids' "hearts" by asking them what they see. You might invite a kid out for a milkshake and ask questions that pertain to her heart:

- What have been the significant joys in your life?
- What have been the significant hurdles in your life?
- What comes naturally to you?
- What do people tell you they most appreciate about you?
- When you're older and look back on your life, what do you want to have done something about?
- What issues in life most concern you?
- Do you feel strongly that you should lead or serve a certain group or type of people?

But don't stop there. Talking with her about her heart is only one piece of the conversation.

FRUIT

In his Sermon on the Mount, Jesus offers this stern warning:

> "Watch out for false prophets. They come to you in sheep's clothing, but inwardly they are ferocious wolves. By their fruit you will recognize them. Do people pick grapes from thornbushes, or figs from thistles? Likewise, every good tree bears good fruit, but a bad tree bears bad fruit. A good tree cannot bear bad fruit, and a bad tree cannot bear good fruit. Every tree that does not bear good fruit is cut down and thrown into the fire. Thus, by their fruit you will recognize them." (Matthew 7:15–20)

In other words, the fruit that your life bears will resemble the life that you live.

When the apostle Paul came along, he didn't want anyone to have to make any assumptions. So he listed the kinds of fruit that believers' lives should yield. Galatians 5:22–23 says: "But the fruit of the Spirit is love, joy, peace, patience, kindness, goodness, faithfulness, gentleness and self-control. Against such things there is no law."

If your teen leaders are passionately dedicated to following Jesus, their lives will display some of these fruits. They have to! You just need to be a fruit inspector and help them understand where they might best fit into ministry leadership.

When I (David) first entered youth ministry, it was on a part-time basis while I was still in college. I took over a group of three kids . . . and one of them was my younger brother. To put it bluntly, we had plenty of room to grow.

Within a matter of months, we were reaching 70 kids a week. I'm hesitant to use numbers because I know there's much more to ministry than how many youth are involved. But I assure you, when God starts using kids to reach other kids, numerical growth just happens. That's why the book of Acts mentions specific numbers and includes comments such as, "And the Lord added to their number daily those who were being saved." (Acts 2:47). Those 70 teenagers represented almost every single teenager in our area; the whole community had only 1,200 people total.

But I wasn't surprised. After all, we had a secret weapon—*Tasha*.

I met Tasha because her parents owned the restaurant where my dad and I liked to meet for lunch. Tasha came from a Roman Catholic background, which was different from my Protestant upbringing and the church where I served. Nonetheless, Tasha quickly found our church to be her spiritual home, and she went to work redecorating our ministry—*with a ton of new kids.*

Tasha had a fairly powerful testimony, and she wasn't timid—*at all*. In fact, I don't think she even knew what the word *timid* meant. She was always thinking about what she could do to allow more of her friends and the people in the community to hear the message of God. So we decided to unleash her on our small town. She designed fliers. She made phone calls. Tasha even invaded the areas where teenagers gathered, be it the park, the bus stop, or the one gas station in town. But wherever she went, Tasha talked about her faith and invited kids to attend our youth ministry.

Tasha played a more significant role in growing our ministry than anyone else in our church—myself included. She was my one-woman evangelism squad. When I left that church, hundreds of kids in that rural county knew about our church and the love of Jesus—all because of Tasha's unabashed efforts to lead her friends to Christ.

I tremble when I think about what would've happened—and all that *wouldn't* have happened—if I'd given Tasha the ill-fitting leadership role of small group teacher or drama team member.

All of your teen leaders have been ordained by God to bear fruit for God's kingdom. It makes sense to plug them into leadership fits where they'll be able to function accordingly. Maybe they've already seen some fruit in their lives; maybe they haven't. But you'll want to talk with them about it, regardless.

If you meet with a teen leader to discuss his fruit, you can ask the following questions to get you going:

- In what ways do you think God works in your life?
- What generally happens when you share your faith? Teach? Pray? Encourage others?
- Has God ever poured out blessings on something you've done for God or offered to God?
- Is there something you're really good at doing?
- Recently, what were some of the ways you were a blessing to others?
- What do other people often tell you that you're good at doing?

These sorts of questions should get kids' juices flowing. They'll also give you an opportunity to get your kids excited about leading in ways that God will strongly bless.

But don't just rely on these questions. Your power of observation is key. Ask yourself: *What fruit do I notice in this teen's life? What do other kids and adult leaders see in this person?*

Fruit is often dangling for all to see.

GOD'S LEADING

Occasionally a kid may approach you and initiate a conversation about his leadership fit. That happened to me (David) just today as I was writing this chapter.

This afternoon Javier and I met over a couple of bacon double cheeseburgers and some Cajun fries at our favorite place across town. Javier is a good-looking, popular, and über-talented college student who's been volunteering with a local, Christian-based, nonprofit organization in my city.

Javier's specialty is rapping—and he's great at it. Let me just tell you—I've seen my fair share of Christian rappers as I've traveled all over for speaking engagements, and much of it is lame. Not so with Javier. He gets invitation after invitation to share his gift in churches and ministries around our city.

At lunch today Javier said he believes God is speaking to him about his future and what he should pursue in college. He told me he enjoys teaching others. (*Yep, that joy shows in his leadership of middle school and high school small groups.*) He also told me he likes leading teenagers. (*I know that's true as well, given how much time he spends volunteering at the local schools.*) And then he told me he wants to get a degree in religious studies and work in an environment where he can impact teenagers' lives.

Knowing what he had in mind, I went ahead and asked, "So what do you think God is leading you to do?"

"I think God wants me in youth ministry."

I don't have a corner on God's will; but if I had to make a call on what God wanted for Javier's life, I'd also say youth ministry.

Rather than tip my hand and give Javier a false leading, I riddled him with questions about his discernment. I asked him whether or not he thought God had called him into ministry, and then I had him explain why he thought so. I talked with him about his background and his past experiences and how they might factor into his decision. I asked him what he thought youth ministry was really about. I asked what he was doing to maintain his relationship with Jesus. We spoke about the monumental ups and the crushing downs that youth pastors experience. Finally, I asked him if he met the standard for being a pastor as outlined in the New Testament.

In short, I grilled him on what he thought God was leading him to do. Knowing Javier's love for Jesus, I gave him a leadership opportunity right away so he could flesh out that calling within our ministry setting to find out whether or not God was indeed leading him to full-time vocational ministry.

It might be rare that a 15-year-old kid would tell you she thinks God is leading her to a career path. More often than not, you'll hear something like, "I sense God is calling me to witness to my friends at school," or, "I feel like God is trying to tell me to step up my faith somehow." If a teen informs you of some sort of leading that she thinks God has for her, don't be afraid to ask her some tough questions. Embrace the fact that God speaks to her about her life and then serve as a point of reference for her in a mentoring role.

If this happens, make sure you talk with the teen about some of the following:

- Why do you think God's leading you along this path?
- Why would God be concerned about that?
- Do you think this is a good thing or a bad thing?
- What will you need to do to accomplish this?
- How will your life be different if you follow God's leading on this?

It's fairly simple to see that ongoing conversations are key to helping teens find their leadership fits. This is just another reason to engage kids in one-on-one relationships: *It blesses your ministry in the long run.*

Let me go ahead and say it because I know somebody reading this book is thinking it: *Can I cover all of this in just one meeting?* No. Don't try to squeeze all of these conversations into one. Discernment is a process and it takes time. Meet with your kids one-on-one and talk with them about their hearts. Then give them some time to reflect on your conversation. You might even want to assign them some Scriptures to read or tasks to perform. If a first conversation with a kid isn't sufficient—and it may not be—then talk with him at a later date about the fruit his life yields . . . and so on.

Don't try to cover all the bases at once. You'll probably either overwhelm your kids or confuse them, and neither suits your purpose.

BE LEERY OF SHORTCUTS

Since we've covered some of the best ways to help teens find their leadership fits, we might as well acknowledge that there are also plenty of ways to cut corners. But I've seen what happens when adult volunteers try to play "pin the fit on the teen," and it's usually not pretty. Here are just a few of the famous—*or infamous*—shortcuts.

"FILL THE HOLES"

A youth pastor has vacancies on the drama team, worship team, and evangelism team. He also has a few kids who say they want to lead. The temptation is to start filling the gaps with the kids whom he believes have what it takes to get the job done, rather then truly discerning who's the right kid for the job.

Let's say he places the outgoing kid on the Campus Evangelism team because it makes sense. But in reality, God's calling that guy to help on the Food/Snack team. The artsy girl he placed on the Drama team is actually destined by God to start a new ministry to visit nursing homes and teach elderly people how to paint.

The list of flubs can go on and on when we practice the "fill the holes" mentality of finding leadership fits. Sure, we'll occasionally get a few of them right. But how much is it costing our ministry, our church, and our community for us to play God?

RELYING SOLELY ON "PERSONAL STRENGTH" INVENTORIES

Youth workers often hand out "personal strengths" workbooks to kids, hoping these booklets will infallibly direct teenagers into their perfect leadership fits by focusing on their strengths.

Take this 10-minute test and—voilà! I found your fit!

I've read the Bible enough to know that if I can identify what my personal strengths are, then I've most likely also identified the ways in which God is probably *not* going to use me. Think about scriptural examples: God often uses people in their weaknesses so there's less of *them* and more of *God*.

Here are a couple of lines God never said: "Moses, you're so good at leading international exiles, I think I'll make you Pharaoh." "Hey, Esther. I'm banking on all of your conflict-resolution skills to handle the evil Haman's genocidal plan." Those sorts of statements from God would be ridiculous. God has a knack for picking the least and the last and the lowliest to do some pretty amazing things.

Proverbs 3:5 clearly says for us to, "Trust in the LORD with all your heart and lean not on your own understanding." If we teach kids to trust in their own personal strengths, they may not trust in God.

In spite of our lofty view of ourselves, the Bible makes it clear that we're actually fairly weak. After battling opposition for some time, the apostle Paul *finally* learned how to cope with his reality in 2 Corinthians 12:9 when God told him, "My grace is sufficient for you, for my power is made perfect in weakness."

If we choose our kids' leadership fits based *only* on their personal strengths, we may find that we're operating our ministry on human ability instead of God's supernatural power.

Personal strength inventories can be great tools. Just remember that they're only *tools*. Don't get so excited about a tool that you forget to invite the Master Carpenter to assist you.

SPIRITUAL GIFTS ASSESSMENTS

Here's another spiritual-sounding solution for discovering a teen's leadership fit. It basically amounts to teenagers answering some questions and filling in a predetermined and corresponding matrix so they can find their "match made in heaven." Spiritual gifts tests use all the right words and phrases, but they may bring about more heartache than help if they're used irresponsibly. We definitely can't just hand a teen a packet, ask her to fill it out, and—BANG!—expect her spiritual gifts to be discovered.

Let's not forget that Paul got as riled up about the misuse and misunderstanding of spiritual gifts as he did when sin was found within the church. If we're to incorporate our kids' spiritual gifts—which is a good and godly thing—we must do so in a biblically accurate manner.

When addressing the subject of spiritual gifts with the congregation in Rome, Paul wrote:

> We have different gifts, according to the grace given to each of us. If your gift is prophesying, then prophesy in accordance with your faith; if it is serving, then serve; if it is teaching, then teach; if it is to encourage, then give encouragement; if it is giving, then give generously; if it is to lead, do it diligently; if it is to show mercy, do it cheerfully. (Romans 12:6–8)

Later in the New Testament, Paul addressed the same subject and offered a more extensive list of gifts (1 Corinthians 12:4–11). Within these two lists, we find such gifts as prophecy, encouraging, showing mercy, healing, speaking in tongues, and others.

But even these lists aren't the Bible's only teaching on the subject; we know the Bible records the Holy Spirit giving believers other types of gifts as well. *But where does the Bible talk about the gift of administering the registration table or participating on the drama team or leading the evangelism group on the school campus?*

Before we just hand kids these packets that are "guaranteed" to help them discover their spiritual gifts, let's invest some time in *teaching* our kids about spiritual gifts. The Bible is clear, but chances are good that your youth will still need your help, leadership, and discernment skills to understand spiritual gifts and their uses. They'll need to know the real purpose behind spiritual gifts, why kids without a relationship with Jesus don't have them, and much more.

I'm not saying that spiritual gift assessments or personal strength inventories are completely valueless. *I'm saying nothing can replace* you *as a discerning mentor in your kids' lives.* Your kids need you—a lot! Don't take any of these shortcuts to find leadership fits; otherwise, you may find yourself facing disappointment more often than you want or should.

FUNCTIONING IN THE FIT

When all is said and done, you'll need to remind your kids (and yourself) that deciding on leadership fits involves some flexibility. Try to get it right as soon as possible, but don't communicate to your kids that it's a "done deal" and they now have to serve in their particular positions of leadership until Jesus returns. Remember to build in some latitude for shifting and tweaking as you go along.

Also, don't forget that as your teens grow in their faith and their leadership abilities, their leadership fits may shift a bit. For example, if someone made a terrific greeter when she was a high school freshman, keep in mind that she might grow in her leadership ability to where she could lead a small group by her junior year.

But once you and your teens agree on their leadership fits, give them a chance to test-drive in those positions. By giving them practice runs, you get a chance to see them function in their leadership fits.

If you've poured into the one-on-one conversations, asked God to guide you, and been up front and honest about the leadership roles, chances are good that you're going to place kids within the leadership fits that will allow them to bless others and be blessed at the same time. But test-drive the decision to help build their confidence and make sure.

For example, if you have a kid who says he wants to lead by caring for others, take him to visit church members in one of the local hospitals and observe him in action. If you've got a teen who believes he's called to teach, let him fill in as a small group leader (under your observation). And don't forget to offer some feedback after each of these opportunities. Those conversations will help you when it comes time to train your leaders, which is what we'll talk about in our next chapter.

Unfortunately, nothing's guaranteed when it comes to helping teens find their leadership fits; I wish it were, but that's just not the case. All we can do is strive to operate as responsibly and biblically as we know how, sharing our discernment with our kids in godly one-on-one relationships.

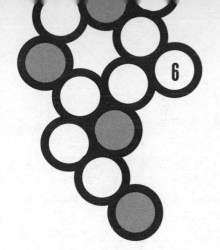

6

IN THE SHADE OF THE GARDENER
TRAINING OUR TEENAGE LEADERS

Both Sandy and Darren had regular contact with new kids. It was common to see each of them connecting with kids on campuses and out in the community. Their efforts—combined with personal invitations, fliers, online social networks, text messages, fun events, and free giveaways—ensured that new kids were always showing up at their respective ministries.

But only Sandy seemed able to hang on to new kids.

Darren always had new faces appearing in his youth ministry, but many kids who visited didn't come back. Consequently, Darren's group never seemed to grow in impact.

Sandy's group, on the other hand, had astronomical growth. Not only were kids putting their trust in Jesus and growing in their faith, but the group as a whole was also growing in number, reaching new kids each week. And these new kids stuck to Sandy's ministry like glue.

The secret to her success wasn't high tech; she just used two different colored nametags *and some well-trained teen leaders*.

When a kid walked into Sandy's ministry, she was greeted by teenagers manning a registration table. These teens asked everyone the same two questions: "What's your name?" and "Is this your first time here?"

If the youth was returning for the second, third, or one hundredth time, she received a green nametag that she could decorate as she wished. And thanks to the alphabetically organized logbook, which was updated each week with newly added names and attendance charts, this process was smooth and quick.

If a kid turned out to be a first-time visitor, the exact same process was followed with one key exception: *The greeters nonchalantly handed him a red nametag instead of a green one.*

When that kid walked into the main room wearing a red nametag, almost instantly, warm and caring teenagers engaged him in conversation, sat at his table during the meal, and hung out with him during worship. Throughout the night those welcoming teenagers would talk with the new guy about his friends, school, family, hobbies, and so on. And all of those pieces of information were used to connect him to other kids with similar interests.

So it was easy to see why first-time visitors to Sandy's ministry became second-time visitors and eventually active members in her youth ministry. All of her teen leaders—from those who ran the registration table to those who comprised the welcome wagon—had been very specifically and intentionally trained to care for anyone new who walked through their doors.

Darren, on the other hand, never methodically trained his teen leaders. And week after week this reality revealed itself.

> Darren, on the other hand, never methodically trained his teen leaders. And week after week this reality revealed itself.

DANGEROUS ASSUMPTIONS

Unfortunately, too many youth workers have adopted the flawed mind-set that restricted the growth potential of Darren's youth ministry. They falsely assume that teen leaders will automatically know what to do, how to do it, and why they're doing it. But that's just not the case.

Successful leaders in world-class organizations never leave their employees' effectiveness to chance. The very first thing they do with new employees is subject them to a battery of training measures. And that strategy isn't restricted to executives at Fortune 500 companies; even teenagers who get paid minimum wage to flip burgers or bag groceries are trained on exactly what to do and how to do it.

The military is another great example of thorough training. Their preparation of new recruits is so intense that they pack them up and send them on an all-expenses-paid, 13-week stay at Camp You-Know-What-on-Earth. That's because no military leader is willing to go into battle with untrained troops. History even shows that forces who were small in number but well-trained have sometimes overpowered larger forces whose training was only moderate.

Training matters in athletics, too. As I (David) write this, the 2008 NCAA Division I champs play football just up the road from me in Gainesville, Florida. These athletes spend hours each day training their bodies and minds for Saturday showdowns on the gridiron. Interestingly their organization has almost as many coaches and trainers as they do football players. But it appears as though their training strategy is paying off. From the 2006 through 2009 seasons, they produced two National Championship teams and one Heisman Trophy winner.

In case any doubts remain about the necessity of training, let me make one final appeal—to Scripture. The Bible offers example after example of godly leaders receiving great training. Moses trained Joshua, Elijah trained Elisha, Jesus trained the disciples, and Paul trained Timothy. Each of these up-and-coming leaders had one thing in common: A leader who invested know-how and love into him.

I think you get my point. Any team or organization that's serious about its purpose trains its people. Since we have the greatest purpose of all—pointing others to Jesus— shouldn't our teen leaders have access to training that's intentional and specific?

If you've read this far, then you're probably convinced by now that teen leaders must first be trained. But how?

MINISTRY TRAINING 101

The more expectations we place on our teen leaders, the more training we must offer them. The tendency in teen leadership training is to begin by showing kids how to use Photoshop to design a slick flier, teaching them how to write and act in dramas in front of the rest of the group, or doing something else that will have a tangible (and positive) effect on our ministries.

But let me ask a couple of questions. If Conner has been trained to share his faith effectively but spends an hour every night clicking through porn sites, have we really created someone who's acceptable for ministry leadership?

> If Conner has been trained to share his faith effectively but spends an hour every night clicking through porn sites, have we really created someone who's acceptable for ministry leadership?

If Caitlyn has been so thoroughly trained that she can manage the teen database in her sleep but doesn't love half of the kids who are listed in it, how far have we really come? If Raul can run the soundboard, fog machines, and video projectors with his eyes closed but continually repels other kids because of his anger and arrogance, are we really better off?

Of course not.

Before we equip our teen leaders with the skills they'll need to lead others in ministry, we must first ensure that they're committed to Jesus and dedicated to living lives worthy of ministry leadership responsibility. While that entails much, the basics include just three crucial elements.

ELEMENT ONE: LIVE LIKE JESUS

A simple look at the Gospels will show how much time Jesus invested in his disciples before entrusting them with ministry. Yes, the good news had to be preached, the sick had to be healed, and churches had to be planted; but Jesus was committed to developing followers whose first obligation was to live like him.

Besides calling each of the disciples into a personal relationship with him—where they'd follow him as their teacher day in and day out—Jesus began his earthly ministry by describing the attitudes and kingdom focus of God's followers (Matthew 5:1–12). In that same address, Jesus trained his disciples on the proper way to pray (Matthew 6:5–13). Then the lessons began to dig a little deeper as Jesus tackled subjects such as forgiveness (Matthew 18:21–35), humility (Matthew 20:20–28), and love (Matthew 22:34–40).

This kind of hands-on training helped ensure the disciples' success with the enormous task Jesus would soon give them. Jesus wasn't willing to spend all of his time on "Demon Exorcism and You" without knowing where each of the disciples' hearts were. So the brunt of his ministry to them was spent patiently teaching and training them to live as he lived.

And the world was changed because of Jesus' strategy.

By the way, isn't the main goal of youth ministry to get kids to live as Jesus did? Then we might as well start there with our teen leaders' training, too.

ELEMENT TWO: LOVE OTHERS

Forget about training teenagers for a moment and let me ask you a question: If you had to choose between a church where the music, technology, and programming were great, but the people were rude, snobby, and basically unloving; or a church where the band, preaching, and activities were mediocre, but the people were genuine, compassionate, and relational—where would you go?

Granted, we don't want to have to choose between these two settings—mainly because our ministries should offer quality *and* love. But I highly doubt you'd settle for very long in a place where love isn't a cornerstone. That's how important love is.

As Jesus' life on earth came to a close, he reminded his disciples of the importance of love:

My command is this: Love each other as I have loved you. Greater love has no one than this: to lay down one's life for one's friends. You are my friends if you do what I command. I no longer call you servants, because servants do not know their master's business. Instead, I have called you friends, for everything that I learned from my Father I have made known to you. You did not choose me, but I chose you and appointed you so that you might go and bear fruit—fruit that will last—and so that whatever you ask in my name the Father will give you. This is my command: Love each other. (John 15:12–17)

Paul echoed similar thoughts in 1 Corinthians 13. (You most likely heard that passage read at the last wedding you attended—*love is patient, kind, not proud*, and so on. If you haven't read this one in a while, you may want to brush up on it.) Paul even went on to say that all of our prophecy, faith, and works are worth *nothing* if we don't have love.

Wow.

Many youth pastors focus on the programming, the lighting, and the energy in the room while neglecting the most essential element of all—love. We can't forget we're in the people business, and all of those people need love—God's love and our love. If we forget this truth, it'll show up in our ministry. We may unknowingly create teen leaders who excel in skills and lack in love.

Does anyone hear a resounding gong . . . or clanging cymbals?

Cool bands, great camps, and fun games are wonderful, but they have nothing on love. Make sure your teen leaders love others.

> ## Cool bands, great camps, and fun games are wonderful, but they have nothing on love. Make sure your teen leaders love others.

ELEMENT THREE: SERVE HUMBLY

Not long ago one of my (David's) teen worship bands became more interested in themselves than in leading worship. They believed they were exempt from the rules, and they acted on that belief—*a lot*. They formed an impenetrable clique that was damaging the atmosphere of love that we were so desperately trying to create. This worship team had more arrogance than '80s rock bands had hair spray. In short, the intoxicating spotlight had made them prideful and egotistical.

I addressed the problem by making it the topic of our devotionals several times; I even issued a few direct warnings, but nothing helped. Finally, I decided they needed a strong dose of humility, and that's what they got.

One day I told the team to wear work clothes to band practice that afternoon, and I received more than a few strange looks when I did so.

When the last band member finally strolled in to practice (tardy enough to be considered fashionably late), I gathered them all together and once again shared my frustrations with them. I also confessed that I'd run out of patience (and Bible verses) to deal with the problem.

Then I marched them outside to a month-old pile of rotten pumpkins that were left over from the annual fundraiser and needed to be placed in the rented dumpster. Shovelful by shovelful, gripe by gripe, the band members learned the hard way that all leaders must serve humbly.

Attitudes changed after that "band practice."

Even the best teen leaders need occasional reminders of their need for humility. Therefore, any teen leadership training must include the necessity of humility as a core value. If not, then we may end up producing arrogant and irrelevant leaders.

Unlike leadership in the world, ministry leadership calls for a servant-minded attitude. The ultimate leader—Jesus—flatly said, "For even the Son of Man did not come to be served, but to serve, and to give his life as a ransom for many" (Mark 10:45). And he backed up that declaration time and time again. For instance, in John 13 he used a towel and a bowl of water to wash his disciples' feet—a task that was reserved for slaves in that day (verses 1–17). And in all of the crucifixion accounts, Jesus humbly endured the ridicule and taunts of those who were conspiring to kill him en route to a horrible death on the cross.

In light of that supreme example, we have the prerogative to ask our teen leaders tough questions:

- [*to drama team members who are used to standing in the spotlight*] Do you feel any obligation to pick up trash after a service?
- [*to verbally gifted leaders*] Can you receive appreciation from others who admire your gifts without letting it all go to your head?
- [*to teens who lead small group sessions*] Do you ever hang around to stack chairs after the program ends?

- [*to teenagers who are really good at sharing their faith*] Can you remain patient with those who are still timid about sharing their faith?

Teen leaders must humbly serve. They can learn humility the easy way—*or on top of Mount Pumpkin.*

Live like Jesus, love others, and *serve humbly.* These elements are certainly crucial parts of a real relationship with Jesus. Once we've spent some time reminding our kids about being devoted to these practices in their faith, it's time to talk about sharing that faith with others.

SHARING YOUR FAITH

In my (Jonathan's) teen leadership programs, evangelism was always the first thing I taught my kids. This team of kids became a huge asset for multiple ministries around Sacramento. We used them as counselors at various citywide evangelism events and at several campus ministry events. Churches and Christian organizations were elated to hear that a team of kids had been trained to share their faith.

The training process was fun. I started by addressing how our "unchurched friends" perceive us. I even came up with four ways to be sure to scare them off. (This creative little training exercise inspired my book titled *Do They Run When They See You Coming?: Reaching Out to Unchurched Teenagers* [Zondervan/Youth Specialties, 2004].)

Then we looked at the biblical mandate to live the gospel in word and action. I used numerous passages to support the main point. One exercise was to take Jesus' command to go and make disciples of all nations (the Great Commission) and lead a discussion as to what "going and making disciples" looks like.

In a recent podcast with my buddy Greg Stier, he elaborated on that biblical text, highlighting the fact that the word *go* in that passage is better translated, "as you are going." The Great Commission was basically Jesus telling us, "As you are going through daily life, be all about making disciples."

I enjoy breaking my kids into smaller groups and asking them to come up with examples of how to do that. Sometimes I ask the groups to create a skit to show what this looks like. This exercise not only makes them understand the passage to the point of application, but it also forces them to come up with real-life examples and then, in essence, practice going and making disciples.

Another week I might divide my youth into groups and put them on the spot by giving them this scenario: "Your friend asks you if you ever think about life after death. The conversation leads her to ask what you believe and how you think someone gets to heaven.

You have an opportunity to share the good news about Jesus with her. Let's hear you tell her the good news right now."

Then I let each person try to explain the gospel to the rest of the group.

This exercise demands a lot of kids, requiring them to search what they know about the gospel and try to verbalize it. Many kids will fail miserably at this (many *adults* will fail miserably at this), but it leaves them wondering, *What should I say?* At this point (now that they're primed), I train them on *what to say*. In other words, I teach them how to share the gospel in a clear, concise, biblical manner.

The following week I hit them with something different: "Okay, now that you know how to share the gospel—the question is, how do you find opportunities 'as you are going' to get from a normal conversation to a spiritual one?"

I always make sure that I connect all of these evangelism exercises and point them back to living as Jesus did. Sharing the gospel must be done in word and action. I'm a big advocate of doing both. After all, if we aren't living as Jesus did, then no one will want to listen to us share about him anyway.

These exercises are fun, and kids walk away feeling better equipped for these kinds of spiritual conversations.

MINISTRY SKILLS

Now that we've covered the essentials common to every teen leader in our ministry, we can turn our attention to training that revolves around teaching individual skills and responsibilities.

Can we train kids how to lead small groups? Absolutely. Can we help them form a worship band? Definitely. Can we show them how to organize a service project to help the needy? Easily. The list goes on and on, but you get the point. Training teens with the skills they'll need to lead in ministry is where the rubber meets the road.

> Training teens with the skills they'll need to lead in ministry is where the rubber meets the road.

Teen leadership programs provide great opportunities to teach these kinds of ministry skills—skills that kids can use both with their friends at school and in the youth room at church.

Let's take those awesome greeters from Sandy's youth ministry, for example. Their job description required them to—

- arrive a half-hour before start time to get set up;
- pray together before the doors opened;
- be friendly with all of the kids who come through the door;
- anticipate—*and meet*—the kids' needs;
- set the tone for love, care, and community;
- accurately record the kids' names (both visitors' and regulars') in the logbook;
- have information available for any parents who should walk in while dropping off a kid;
- know the facility inside and out so directions can be given to first-timers; and
- return the logbook to Sandy's office and clean up after registration ends.

Sandy wanted something more than a couple of kids standing at the front door and slapping high-fives with the kids they were comfortable with. She knew that the more she expected of her teen leaders, the more she'd have to train them. So she did.

Remember—this is just the greeters' job description. If you have a worship team, office support personnel, publicity team, or campus outreach team, then you'll need to create accurate and detailed job descriptions for each of those teams as well. More importantly, you'll need to make time to show the kids exactly what each of those responsibilities means and includes. Finally, you must teach them why every single one of their duties is important to the ministry.

Training teen leaders should also include some time that's dedicated to building unity. We won't focus on it here because we've written an entire chapter about this integral process (chapter 7). But suffice it to say, you'll need to make sure there's harmony among team members and unity among the different teams, too. You want to build one teenage leadership ministry, not a bunch of groups who do their own things.

Finally, training should involve actual practice of some kind. Most sports teams don't consider their preparation complete until they've played a scrimmage. A scrimmage lets the team try out what they've been learning without risking an official loss. Youth ministries can scrimmage, too.

For instance, to make sure the Greeter team is working smoothly, host a mock youth group night and have some "guinea-pig kids" practice registering (as regular attendees *and* first-time visitors). To get the most out of this practice session, secretly tell a couple of the guinea pigs to pretend to have problems that need to be solved by the greeters. Also assign a few unexpected questions that the guinea pigs can ask the greeters.

To ensure that the Food/Snack team knows how to feed the masses, you might have them prepare something for an adult Sunday school class. (Not only would that let them practice, but it would also score big points with the adults!) You can come up with similar ways to allow the other teen leadership teams to practice their jobs.

This strategy is low-risk and gives every teen leadership team a chance to function as they've been trained. More importantly, it also gives you a chance to see them in action before anything is on the line. And this kind of training isn't complete until you've debriefed with each team or individual team leader on how they did and how they can improve.

If you want to up the ante a little bit, you can always do a "soft opening." A little more risk is involved in this kind of training, but the upside is that you get to see your teen leaders in action. To do a soft opening, you might want to invite only the kids from within your youth ministry before taking it to the streets. This is just another way to practice doing ministry on our "siblings in Jesus Christ" before we take it to the world.

Here are other ways to practice: You can line up service projects at the homeless shelter in your area, the orphanage up the street, or even the food pantry that operates out of your church. Not only does this help build unity, but it also helps ensure that you've got kids who want to lead others by serving them.

Regardless of the strategies you employ, give your team(s) a couple of chances to practice what you've been training them to do. This will increase their confidence—and yours.

TRAINING RESOURCES

Okay, you're probably thinking, *All of this sounds great, but how do I get from where I'm at to where I want to be?*

Fortunately, there are tons of ways that you can provide training to your newly chosen team(s) of teenage leaders. The rest of this chapter identifies some of the most practical ways you can do this, and it also explains the advantages and disadvantages of each strategy.

PROFESSIONAL TRAINERS

These are folks who train or consult with churches for a living. Both of us lead dozens of training sessions in churches all around the country each year. To take advantage of this kind of training, all you have to do is get your teen leaders to show up on a Saturday for a workshop and lunch and then let the trainer do the rest. This is probably the easiest way to do training, as it requires the least amount of work from you, the youth pastor or leader.

Bringing in a professional does require some budget, however. So our suggestion is to use this type of training as you can afford it, maybe once a year. Yes, it's great; but you can train your own teen leaders throughout the year using some other, more affordable ways.

WEEKEND RETREAT

A focused overnighter or weekend training session is tough to beat. It gets you some quality time with your teen leaders, it (usually) costs less than bringing in a professional trainer, and you can focus on the exact needs of your group. Plus, it allows for some fun and relaxation, too. And these venues allow you and your teams to set ministry goals (both quantitative and qualitative) for the upcoming months.

Veteran youth workers have found they can comfortably and effectively squeeze four different training sessions into a Friday afternoon through Sunday morning weekend retreat. As powerful as these weekends are, they do require some preparation. You've got cabins or lodges to reserve, meals to line up, training sessions to write, permission slips to retrieve and file, and adult leaders to line up. But the rewards are great. These kinds of weekends are definitely worth your time and effort.

Does this sound like a lot of work?

How about we make your job a little easier by providing you with the complete outline of the training sessions you'll lead that weekend? The Appendix contains a complete agenda and lesson plan for a weekend retreat focused on training your teen leaders.

REGULAR MEETINGS

Of course, you have other cheap and easy options for training your teen leaders. If you want to train your leadership team(s) without the expense of hiring professional trainers or the hassle of organizing a weekend retreat, you can easily do effective training yourself by using regularly scheduled meetings.

I (Jonathan) helped facilitate a teen leadership program at my church where we met once a month after the Sunday services. We provided lunch for everyone and then ran our team meeting from 1 to 3 p.m.

Typically, after a quick team-building activity to break the ice, I'd dedicate about 30 minutes to training the kids. I usually did this myself. Here are a few of the strategies I used.

1. Article, Book, or Podcast Discussion

Training your leaders can be as simple as handing out an article and discussing it as a group. If you meet weekly or monthly, distribute a printed copy of an article to everyone, instruct them to read it right then and there (because oftentimes if you send it home with the kids in advance, some won't read it ahead of time anyway), and then take a few minutes to ask five or six questions about the article.

Let's say the article is about academic cheating—a big problem for an overwhelming majority of teens these days. Your training could include these discussion questions:

- What does the Bible say about cheating?
- What are some ways that we as leaders can avoid academic cheating?
- What are the costs associated with academic cheating?
- What's our responsibility in terms of reporting academic cheating?
- How can our ministry offer help to teens who feel tempted to cheat academically or have already done so?

Of course, this particular training has little to do with "101 Ways to Share Your Faith"—but it has everything to do with living as Jesus did, one of our core values for all teen leaders.

From studies about teens' lives to stories about their actions, you can easily find several articles, reports, or stats to use in your training discussions. You may want to subscribe to a few online youth ministry newsletters and keep your eyes open for relevant articles in newspapers and periodicals. One thing's for sure: Teenagers are always making the news.

Change it up every once in a while and require your teen leaders to listen to a podcast during the week and be ready to discuss it at the training meeting the following Sunday. There are tons of them related to Christian ministry. Then write some discussion questions just as you would for an article or a book. Some kids might enjoy discussing something they *hear* more than something they *read*.

One helpful aspect of this training method is the minimal amount of prep time required. You just need to find an appropriate article or podcast, read or listen to it ahead of time, and then prepare five or six good questions that make *one single point*. The less you talk, the better. This method is more facilitating than training.

2. Ministry or Program Debriefing

Every time we (David) did something in our youth ministry, we discussed it immediately after it ended. Whether it was our weekly outreach ministry, our weekly worship night, or a weekend event, our teen leaders knew the job wasn't finished until we'd debriefed. (Although very occasionally, such as after a really big event like a summer camp, we'd take a couple of days to collect our thoughts before debriefing.)

During this debriefing time, our team of leaders would simply gather around and talk about what just happened—what they liked and didn't like, what they saw, who they spoke with during the relationship-building moments, what could be improved, any special needs within the lives of the kids, and anything else they'd noticed. And then we always wrapped it up with prayer.

The good thing about debriefing on the spot is that the ministry or program is fresh on the leaders' minds. If you delay sharing this information, you risk forgetting something important. Besides, kids are usually willing to hang around and share their thoughts on the advancement of the ministry.

Here are a few pointers to make the most out of your debriefing time:

- *Ask specific questions.* Don't just say, "What did you notice?" Break the ministry down into sections and talk about each piece, one at a time. If you want helpful answers, ask focused questions. Try to be as precise as a doctor or car mechanic when asking these diagnostic questions.
- *Give everyone a chance to talk.* Make sure you don't stifle the group or unnecessarily hurry it. Don't be afraid to call someone's name and ask her a pointed question. "Leigh Ann, you were by the snack bar all night. Could you easily communicate with the other kids, or was the music too loud?"
- *Start with the newest teen leader first.* The military uses this tactic. They tend to start their discussions by asking for feedback from the junior officers first so they won't simply agree with the older officers. But this works well for other reasons, too. The newest leaders will probably bring the freshest set of eyes to the ministry. Further, knowing their opinions are valued will give them some comfort about sharing with the group in the weeks and months ahead.

This sort of training costs nothing and no preparation is required. The only downside is that sometimes—especially if it's after a big event—the leaders may be a bit tired. If that's the case, be sensitive and wise—just ask for thoughts via email or a phone call sometime during the next few days.

3. Team Builders

Building unity was already mentioned once in this chapter, and since all of chapter 7 focuses on this subject, I won't say much here. But just know that getting your team together for some fun, challenging, and interactive team building definitely counts as training. Your teenage leaders will love this stuff—especially if you mix it with lots of food! We provide you with a bunch of team-building ideas in chapter 7 as well.

4. One-on-One

I saved the best kind of regular meetings for last. These cost nothing, other than an occasional milkshake or taco, and require very little preparation. However, they do require some time *during* the training. But one-on-one meetings provide the most effective and impactful form of youth training by far.

I'm talking about one-on-one training between you and a teen leader—not via email, texting, or phone calls, but good old-fashioned face-to-face training.

There's a saying in the South: "Rosebushes grow the best in the shade of the gardener." Of course, rosebushes don't actually grow well in the shade—they need sunlight as every other plant does. The point is, when the presence of the gardener is close and constant, the rosebush is getting the best care. That's what one-on-one training gives your teen leaders: Your close and constant care.

One-on-one training sessions usually deal with far more than ministry; oftentimes they can be used to discuss life or family or faith or whatever else is on the kid's heart. I've seen one-on-one training sessions help discouraged kids regain their fervor for ministry. I've even been blessed to see young people emerge from these kinds of one-on-one relationships to go in search of full-time ministry leadership.

Max, my pastor and mentor, once told me a story about a young man named Randy in whom he'd invested some one-on-one training when he was a youth pastor back in the day.

The church Max served had an old (antique) soda machine that the adults let the youth ministry use. Max joked that the proceeds collected from the drink machine were used to pay his salary. As youth pastor, it was Max's job was to make sure the machine was stocked with drinks, had the appropriate change inside, and was in operating condition. It wasn't a tough job, but it was time-consuming and hindered him from doing other, more important tasks.

So Max asked Randy (one of the middle school kids in Max's youth ministry) if he'd take ownership of the soda machine. To Max's relief, Randy accepted the high priestly duty of taking care of the soda machine.

Max went on to say how much *more* time he'd had to spend on that stupid soda machine when Randy first took it over. First, Max had to go pick up Randy and drive him back to the church. Then Max had to show Randy how to open the machine and take inventory of which drinks needed to be restocked. Of course, Randy also needed to know how to restock it, so that meant a trip to the supermarket for more bottles of soda. Next, Max showed Randy how to count the money and write up a deposit slip for the bank. Yep, you guessed it—Max would then take Randy to the bank so he could make the deposit. Finally, Max drove Randy home. During all of this face time, Max asked questions and made observations that helped him discern whether or not Randy could be trusted with an obligation requiring counting and depositing money.

It wasn't always such a time-intensive task; eventually, Randy learned the ropes and was able to do the entire job by himself. Plus, there were two terrific outcomes to Max's personal investment in Randy. First, Max was finally able to break away from all interaction with the soda machine because Randy became self-sufficient. Second, Randy became a pastor (and remains one to this day), pouring into the lives of others because he once had someone do that for him.

Be warned: One-on-one training is the most time-intensive of all the methods. But there's nothing like doing life with someone as you train her how to share her faith, lead worship, or count the quarters from a soda machine.

With the exception of debriefing, these regular meetings typically work best when food is involved. And the last time I checked, kids like to eat. So provide some food and use one of these training measures to make your team of teen leaders better.

Training is vital for your teen leaders. Now you have a few ideas for how to get it done. But training a team doesn't automatically make it a cohesive team. So let's look at how we can build unity among the kids on our teen leadership team.

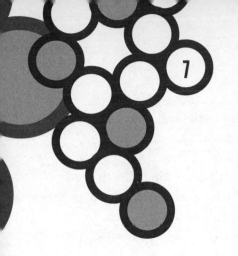

BEYOND "KUMBAYA"

BUILDING AND MAINTAINING UNITY AMONG TEENAGE LEADERS

You usually have a three-hour window each year when all of your kids love each another. Though it's a short moment in time, it's magical nonetheless. All of your kids are embracing each other, offering affirmations and encouragement to one another, and speaking of their genuine and undying love for their fellow youth.

You know what I'm talking about: That last night of summer camp around the bonfire, a time when youth groups used to sing "Kumbaya" (now some slow songs by Chris Tomlin).

Ahhhh. What a perfect way to spend a Saturday night before the long bus ride home on Sunday.

Then Tuesday afternoon hits.

You walk into your office after grabbing some lunch at your favorite fast-food place, and Christy is waiting for you . . . impatiently . . . with her arms crossed menacingly. You know something's up and finally decide against faking a bad case of indigestion so you can hear her out.

For the next half-hour, Christy verbally slams her best friend, Jessica, for something she found written about her on Jessica's Facebook profile. It's one "I can't believe she did that!" after another. Throughout her rant you can't get a word in edgewise.

It quickly dawns on you, *Wait a second. Just 48 hours ago, Christy was after Jessica's heart. Now she's after her throat!*

That experience—and all the rest just like them—makes you wonder if it's truly possible for kids to love one another in biblical unity, let alone lead together in a state of godly harmony.

Well, the good news is, *they can*.

But let me (David) go ahead and say it now: You need to realize that building and maintaining unity among your teen leaders is a multifaceted endeavor. Yes, your Worship team members need to get along with each other (as individuals on the same team), but the Worship team (as a whole) needs to function in tandem with other whole teams—for instance, the Technology and Sound team. Beyond that, every individual teen and every teen leadership team will need to be in step with you and the other adult volunteers.

If you're tempted to throw up your hands at this point—*don't*!

You can use plenty of methods to build and maintain authentic unity among your teenage leaders. This chapter offers not only some biblical principles concerning unity, but also several ways that you can initiate and sustain unity on your team(s). Finally, we provide you with some fun, hands-on, and impactful team-building resources to help you jump-start the unity-building process in your ministry.

THE DISTRACTION OF DISAGREEMENT . . . AND THE BEAUTY OF UNITY

I don't know anybody in youth ministry who leads teams of kids who *always* function in unadulterated unity. Even the best of the best have incidental eruptions of discord on their teams. No one is exempt from having to deal with the distractions caused by disagreement. Even leaders in the Bible sometimes found themselves in similar predicaments.

Take Paul, for example. His writings are littered with exhortations to love one another, care for each other, and exist in unity for Jesus' sake. Perhaps Paul's soapbox is clearest in his letter to the church at Philippi. Throughout this short letter, he dropped phrases such as "being like-minded, having the same love, being one in spirit and of one mind" (Philippians 2:2).

But just in case his target audience didn't catch his drift, Paul singled out a couple of women and called them into account for their public disagreement. At the close of his letter, he wrote:

> Therefore, my brothers and sisters, you whom I love and long for, my joy and crown, stand firm in the Lord in this way, dear friends!
>
> I plead with Euodia and I plead with Syntyche to be of the same mind in the Lord. Yes, and I ask you, my true companion, help these women since they have contended at my side in the cause of the gospel, along with Clement and the rest of my co-workers, whose names are in the book of life. (Philippians 4:1–3)

I don't know what those women were upset about (besides their names), but the fact remains: Their disagreement has been immortalized for two millennia in the Bible. When we all get to heaven, we'll eventually bump into Euodia and Syntyche, and it'll come up. "Oh, you're *that* Euodia and *that* Syntyche." Might be a little awkward.

But dealing with strife on the team is usually awkward.

Unity, on the other hand, is as peaceful as a Sunday afternoon nap. Psalm 133 declares—

How good and pleasant it is when God's people live together in unity!

It is like precious oil poured on the head, running down on the beard, running down on Aaron's beard, down on the collar of his robe.

It is as if the dew of Hermon were falling on Mount Zion. For there the LORD bestows his blessing, even life forevermore.

No one is certain exactly whom King David had in mind when he penned this short psalm 3,000 years ago. But we're now his audience and should comply with his teaching. He doesn't merely talk about the benefit of God's people *avoiding arguments*; he goes one better and says blessings actually come from *living together in unity.* That's an important distinction!

Then David goes on to describe God's blessings on those who live in unity. Granted, we might not fully grasp all of the imagery used in this Jewish psalm, which includes oil, Aaron's beard, and Mount Zion. But the main point is clear: Those who live together in unity will be blessed.

I (David) would go a step further and say that those who live together in unity are not only blessed by God, but also serve as blessings to the people around them. One of my favorite topics to teach on is unity within the church. When I'm invited to speak somewhere and the youth pastor hasn't yet nailed down the theme or asks me if God is leading me in a particular direction, I usually suggest that we center on the topic of unity because it's so desperately needed.

Sometimes I lead a fun, interactive exercise with the kids (depending on the size of the crowd) and have five-person teams work together to construct different shapes and configurations with their bodies. In every one of the structures, teens must contort themselves, lift someone, brace somebody else, and work together to build a human pyramid or other arrangement.

After the fun stuff, we talk about how the activity is like their ministries. The parallel is usually obvious to everyone—it takes all five team members working together in unity to form the shapes and structures. The same is true in ministry: If the team isn't working together in unity, it crumbles and falls. And with that failure come too many costly expenses.

This is the same message that Paul had in mind when he gives the Corinthians the following lesson:

Just as a body, though one, has many parts, but all its many parts form one body, so it is with Christ. For we were all baptized by one Spirit so as to form one body— whether Jews or Gentiles, slave or free—and we were all given the one Spirit to drink. Even so the body is not made up of one part but of many.

Now if the foot should say, "Because I am not a hand, I do not belong to the body," it would not for that reason cease to be part of the body. And if the ear should say, "Because I am not an eye, I do not belong to the body," it would not for that reason cease to be part of the body. If the whole body were an eye, where would the sense of hearing be? If the whole body were an ear, where would the sense of smell be? But in fact God has placed the parts in the body, every one of them, just as he wanted them to be. If they were all one part, where would the body be? As it is, there are many parts, but one body.

The eye cannot say to the hand, "I don't need you!" And the head cannot say to the feet, "I don't need you!" On the contrary, those parts of the body that seem to be weaker are indispensable, and the parts that we think are less honorable we treat with special honor. And the parts that are unpresentable are treated with special modesty, while our presentable parts need no special treatment. But God has put the body together, giving greater honor to the parts that lacked it, so that there should be no division in the body, but that its parts should have equal concern for each other. If one part suffers, every part suffers with it; if one part is honored, every part rejoices with it. (1 Corinthians 12:12–26)

So we know unity is important, but we still don't necessarily know how to build it.

A STRANGE CONSTRUCTION SITE

At some point in our lives, we've all seen the construction process of a home or building. We might drive by it every day en route to work or school, or it may be next door to our own home. But with every passing day, the structure changes and it becomes clearer and clearer what the architect had in mind.

That's not necessarily the case when it comes to building unity. Yeah, we know what we want it to look like when we're done, but building unity isn't as straightforward as building a house, a bank, or a fast-food place. For starters, no matter how hard we work, we can't dictate when unity will be complete. To some degree that's up to our kids. Further, some phases are more difficult than others. Getting kids to learn each other's names in the beginning stage is pretty easy; getting them to trust each other is altogether different. Finally, and unfortunately, there can be all sorts of setbacks to the building process that might wreak havoc on the framework you've worked so hard to build.

So how do we build this obtuse structure called "unity"?

Following are some of the practices that have helped us build and maintain unity among teen leaders, from framework to finish.

1. TEACH ON THE IMPORTANCE OF UNITY

Paul's picture of the church from 1 Corinthians 12 offers a fantastic example that we can use to build and maintain unity among our teen leaders. You'll need to address this topic often as you coach your individual leaders, the leadership teams, and the entire leadership program.

Question the kids about what unity looks like. Speak with them about what happens—or doesn't happen—when discord sneaks into the ministry. Share biblical examples that illustrate the importance of leading together. Make sure they understand God's expectations of them to live and serve in unity.

Finally, you may want to address the fact that even though there are 4 or 7 or 13 different teams of teen leaders, you still have only one youth ministry. As Paul says, there's an eye, a nose, a hand, and an ear, but only one body. This truth has tons of implications that you can explore out loud with your teen leaders. Do so often.

2. CREATE OPPORTUNITIES TO PRACTICE UNITY

Last summer I (David) had the opportunity to speak at one of my favorite camps (that I've been to many times), and for a group of youth workers who wanted to offer their kids something special by connecting an activity with my talk. Being familiar with the campground, it was easy for me to help them out.

We decided that one of the messages would be centered on working together in unity. Since this particular camp has high ropes courses, paintball fields, bridges, outdoor chapels, winding mountain creeks, and much, much more, we resolved to use these identifiable landmarks as part of a camp-wide scavenger hunt one night.

All the teens were grouped into teams, and we gave each team a sheet of paper with several cryptic clues written on it. Though not every team had to go to the same exact landmarks, all of the teams did have to do the same amount of interpretation, searching, and running. Also, all of the teams had to gather at the same ending spot—if they followed their maps correctly.

This crazy little exercise required the teams to work together to interpret clues, navigate difficult terrain, and eventually find the final destination as a group.

That scavenger hunt set us up for a perfect lesson on working together. To this day, whenever I chat with those youth workers, they talk about how exciting and memorable their youth thought that activity and lesson were.

You don't have to rent a camp or hire a speaker to pull off something similar to the experience I just described. You can devise something fairly simple (at a local mall, perhaps) to build unity or put a challenge before your team(s) for them to conquer together. (And we've provided a few ideas later in this chapter.) Either way, you'll build unity through the experiences.

Teen leaders can also practice unity by serving together. Put your kids in teams and send one group to a homeless shelter to help clean, another group to an orphanage to love on orphans, and a third group to a soup kitchen to serve dinner. (Resist the urge to send a group of kids to your house to mow!)

Serving together—and suffering together—creates relational bonds. Put your leaders in situations where they must work together for the benefit of others. At its core that's what a teenage leadership ministry is anyway.

Although I parodied summer camp's "Kumbaya" moments, the truth is that those kinds of experiences usually lend themselves to building unity. And it's easy to see why this is the case. At overnighters, weekend retreats, weeklong camps, and short-term mission trips, kids are *doing life* together. They're sharing the exact same circumstances, challenges, opportunities, teachings, and purpose. Those common joys—and sufferings—unite them.

We constantly need to create opportunities to practice unity.

3. RE-CREATE MOMENTS OF UNITY-BUILDING SUCCESS

If you notice that a particular challenge or teaching or experience fosters unity among your team(s), re-create it in varying ways to get the most out of it. In other words—if something works, throw a different cover on it and do it again!

If you notice your team responds well to a specific teaching style or way of serving together, reuse the same methodology. Maybe you're teaching teen leaders how to work as a team by solving a problem together. Hand each group of teen leaders a slip of paper containing a hypothetical real-life problem that could occur in their group: Jessica has come to the group for three weeks in a row and never feels accepted. Her mom mentioned to another mom that Jessica won't be coming back to church anymore because she said it's the last place she wants to be. What do you do?

Or maybe this one: Austin is on the teen leadership team. Craig, another teen leader, just found out that Austin got his girlfriend pregnant. Austin doesn't drive, so he asked Craig if he could drive Austin and his girlfriend to an abortion clinic. What should Craig do?

Um . . . that last one will be interesting.

After doing an activity like this, listen to the feedback. Did kids not only learn from it, but also enjoy it? Did it draw them closer and help them make decisions or resolve problems as a team? If you find it worked well, use the same method again. This doesn't mean never try anything else. Just don't be afraid to continue using a tool that works.

Also keep in mind that some kids will respond better to challenges, and some will respond better to teaching or instruction. So you'll want to tailor the experiences to your particular youth.

4. MAKE EVERY TEEN LEADER RESPONSIBLE FOR MAINTAINING THE UNITY THAT'S BEEN BUILT

Did you notice what the apostle Paul told the church in Philippi regarding Euodia and Syntyche? He pulled in some other folks and told them to jump into the ruckus that was already brewing. Read it again: "I plead with Euodia and I plead with Syntyche to be of the same mind in the Lord. Yes, and I ask you, my true companion, help these women . . ." (Philippians 4:2–3).

There's plenty of speculation as to who this "true companion" really was. It could've been Silas, Epaphroditus, Timothy, or someone else altogether. Regardless of the true companion's identity, Paul was asking for some help in maintaining the church's unity.

You can do the same. Inform your kids that it's their responsibility to help resolve conflicts through peaceful, loving, and gracious solutions. If they hear some gossip, they should not only *not repeat it*, but also tactfully challenge the person who initiated the sinful talk. If one of your teen leaders discovers that a fellow leader is having a tough time at home, he should be proactive and approach the hurting one as soon as possible to offer help.

When I first stepped into youth ministry, I went to work building teen leaders right away. (Not because I was instantly wise, mind you—my mentor just informed me that it was one of the biggest pieces of my job!) Things went pretty well at first, but I must confess that building unity among the kids was a time-consuming task. And then one day a monumental dispute erupted and ripped a couple of my teenage leaders apart.

I soon realized that what I'd worked for months to build could be torn down in a single bitter sentence.

I instantly put my teen leaders on *unity-protection patrol*. I informed them that I'd be just as upset with someone who saw or heard something that would disrupt our unity and did nothing about it, as I would be with those who actually caused the disunity.

I'd be just as upset with someone who saw or heard something that would disrupt our unity and did nothing about it, as I would be with those who actually caused the disunity.

Then we talked about what unity protection looks like. We discussed how the people who need the most monitoring are *ourselves*. That's right. What's worse than a bunch of hall monitors walking around, pointing their fingers at others, and saying, "Stop being divisive!" Rather humorous, if you think about it. It would be ironic if the very act of searching for disunity created division in our group.

So my kids began looking for temptations that caused division. They primarily monitored themselves, and then we worked through how to approach someone who was being divisive—how to stifle disunity without creating division. This proactive teaching really helped us protect the unity we'd worked so hard to cultivate.

5. PRACTICE TEAM BUILDING

Okay, it might sound like a no-brainer, but it's one of the easiest ways to build unity and teamwork.

When one youth pastor uses the term *team builder*, she might have a trip to the local ice-cream parlor in mind. Another youth pastor may use the phrase *team builder* to describe a prepared activity or experience that teaches a specific strength or skill. Thus, defining exactly what a team builder looks like can be a tricky task—*so I won't*. I'll just focus on what they do: *Promote unity and teamwork among your ministry leaders.*

Here is a collection of our favorite team-building activities to get you started. Each one comes with a list of required supplies and a detailed description of what you need to do. Don't forget to have plenty of adult volunteers on hand. Besides adding safety and security to your plans, they'll strengthen their relationship with the teen leaders by showing up.

EGG TOWER
Supplies needed:

- Newspaper (lots of it)
- Cellophane tape
- Raw eggs (one per group)

This is a great team builder because athleticism isn't a requirement; absolutely everybody in your group can participate.

Simply divide your group into equal teams—no more than four people on a team. Give each team the same amount of newspaper, the same amount of tape, and one egg. Team members must work together in the time allotted to build a tower that will support the weight of their egg. The team with the tallest tower—that can stand on its own power and still hold the egg—is the winner.

NOTE: It's best to give the teams about four minutes at the beginning to brainstorm their plans and then about 10 minutes to pull it off. Also, make sure you've got some cleaning supplies; you'll probably need it after this exercise.

PILE-UP

Supplies needed:

• One twin-sized bedsheet for each team

Divide your group into several 10-person teams and give each team a twin-sized bedsheet. Have the groups lay their sheets flat on the ground and then tell them that the entire team must stand all of the way on the sheet simultaneously—no one may touch any part of the ground that's not covered by the sheet.

Next, have the team members step off the sheet, fold it in half lengthwise, and lay it back down on the ground. Now instruct them to get their full team back onto the sheet. Once again the entire team must stand on the sheet with no one touching any part of the ground that's not covered by the sheet.

Keep repeating the process to make it increasingly difficult. The goal is to see which team can get their entire group on the smallest area of sheet. Inform them that they can do whatever it takes to fit their group on the sheet, even if it means holding each other or piling on top of each other.

Teams can't be successful without the full cooperation and trust of every team member. They'll need each other: Some for creativity, some for leadership, some for coordination, and some for pure strength.

NOTE: You can also add the element of time and run it as a competition. After each round, eliminate the team that took the longest to get their whole team on top of the bedsheet.

CONTINUED ON NEXT PAGE

OVER THE TOP
Supplies needed:

- Rope
- Bedsheets, enough to build a "wall" in your room (preferred, but not essential)
- Two poles or trees to string a rope between

String a rope about six feet high between two posts or trees. Then hang the bedsheets over the rope to simulate a wall. Now tell your entire teen leadership team to get everyone over the top and on the other side of the rope—without touching the rope or sheet.

The object is simple—the team builder isn't. The first person and last person usually prove to be the most difficult.

Rules

1. No one can touch the rope.
2. No one can go around the end posts. The only way to get to the other side is over the top.
3. No one can reach under the rope to help others up or down. Remember, the sheet and rope represent an imaginary wall. (Hanging the sheet over the rope helps make it look more like an actual wall.)

NOTE: Be conscious of which kids you have participate in this team builder. If some of them are overweight, they may feel awkward.

LAND MINES
Supplies needed:

- Blindfolds
- Water balloons

Set up a "minefield" by randomly placing filled water balloons on a section of ground outside. (Yeah, we need to say *outside* because someone will be tempted to do this in the sanctuary or pastor's office.) A concrete slab or basketball court works great for this team builder. (Grass also works, but you'll need to set boundaries.)

Divide your teen leaders into five-person teams and give each team one blindfold. Instruct the teams to choose one person from their group to wear the blindfold.

The object of this team builder is for the *entire* team to get from one side of the "minefield" to the other the fastest, and with the fewest casualties. The team members who can see must help their blindfolded compatriot navigate the land mines and make it safely to the other side.

Rules

1. If any person on the team touches a mine, she's out. (If the water balloon bursts on her, it just makes it more fun.)
2. The blindfolded team members crossing the minefield must stay within the set boundaries.
3. Only one person per team may be on the minefield at a time.
4. Non-blindfolded team members are *not* allowed to lead their blindfolded teammates by touch; they can only help each other by shouting directions.

NOTE: This team builder is a lot of fun, but it requires a lot of setup on the front end. Also, it works best if the land mines are positioned very close together. You can accomplish this by using a lot of water balloons or by having a slightly smaller area than is comfortable—or both. This will put the teams closer together, thus making the field more difficult to navigate. If you're really sneaky, you might want to employ a few adult leaders (who aren't participating) to sporadically shout out incorrect directions to blindfolded kids.

HUMAN KNOTS
Supplies needed:

- None

Get your group of teen leaders bunched up in a tight circle and tell them to grab the hands of two different people who are *not* standing next to them. In other words,

CONTINUED ON NEXT PAGE

each kid will be holding the hands of two different people. The group will look like a tangled mess, but that's what you want.

Now instruct them to untangle themselves without letting go of each other's hands. It may take them a little while to be successful, but it's possible.

THE GREAT MATTRESS RUN
Supplies needed:

- One twin-sized mattress for every team
- One map for every team

This team builder is so much fun that you might forget that you're actually working. Teams of kids have to carry a mattress a mile or two across town without getting caught by hunters. *Um . . . let me explain.*

While still at the church (or base of your choice), divide the group into five-person teams and give each team a mattress. Next, load up the mattress-equipped teams in minivans, drive them a set distance away from the church (base) in *different* directions, and drop them off. Make sure the distance from the church (base) is exactly the same, or else it's unfair. Somewhere between one and two miles is quite sufficient.

The teams' objective is to be the first group to get from their designated drop-off point back to the church (base) with their mattress.

It may sound easy, but don't forget about the "hunters." The hunters are adult leaders in vehicles who are patrolling the neighborhoods in the designated area of play. If the hunters catch a team, they're able to "tranquilize" the team by making them lie down on their mattress for two minutes.

A team is only safe from the hunters if the entire team is jumping up and down on the mattress. So during their trek back to base, teams need to keep their eyes open for hunters. If a team sees them coming, they should immediately throw down their mattress and start jumping on it.

Rules

1. Teams are only vulnerable to hunters within 100 yards. (The hunters are the judges of this distance.)

2. Hunters can't "stalk" individual teams; they must continue driving around, looking for different teams.

NOTE: For safety reasons, you'll probably need to make sure there are two hunters in every vehicle. That way one can drive while the other is looking for the teams. Don't forget to provide the hunters with video cameras, the footage makes a great video!

ENCOURAGING YARN
Supplies needed:

• Yarn

If you have a group of more than 30 teen leaders, break them in half. Otherwise, just have them sit in a circle facing each other. Make sure your adult leaders are also spread throughout the circle(s).

Next, hand one kid a ball of yarn. Tell her to toss it to someone else in the circle while holding on to the end of the yarn. When the other person catches it, the thrower says something encouraging to that person. ("You're a loyal friend." "You give grace to others." "You're a helpful person.")

Afterward the person who was just encouraged grabs the piece of yarn *in one hand* and tosses the ball of yarn to another person *using his other hand*. He then tells the new person an encouraging point about *her*.

This process can continue for as long as you want. Meanwhile, a spider web of yarn has been created between the kids and adults in the circle. (By the way, the same person can be encouraged more than once and by more than one person.)

The only stipulation for this team builder is that the group must be genuine with each other. They can have fun while doing this, but they need to be serious when they encourage others. Also, don't let the encouragements become simple compliments such as, "I like the way you dress." Force the kids to reach for deeper meaning behind a person, her nature, or her actions.

Be watchful of newer teen leaders who aren't as well known by the group. You may want to privately ask an adult leader or a great "inner circle" kid to focus on the new leader.

CONTINUED ON NEXT PAGE

When everyone has had at least one turn encouraging and being encouraged, lead a discussion about the activity while everyone holds on to the yarn (keeping the spider web intact).

Possible questions to ask:

1. Did you learn something about someone else? If so, what?
2. How did the activity make you feel?
3. How important do you think we are to one another?
4. Do you think the people in our circle spoke the truth about each other?
5. What does this tell us about the community we have?
6. How can we encourage each other in the future *without* using yarn?

When or if the discussion dies down, take a pair of scissors and cut a few connections between kids. Then discuss the effect(s) that this action has on the group.

NOTE: Throughout the team builder, make sure only one person is talking at a time. Side conversations will make this activity last too long, and it won't allow everyone to receive a few seconds of special encouragement.

BLIND SQUARE
Supplies needed:

- A blindfold for every teen leader
- One large rope, at least 40 feet in length

Simply blindfold all of your teen leaders and then throw a rope on the ground next to them. Tell them to pick up the rope and make a square using the full length of it. Give them no further instructions.

There's no trick; it's just great to see who takes charge, how the kids organize the corners, how they talk to one another, if one person facilitates from the middle, and so on.

CRASH

Supplies needed:

- Blindfolds (one for every five teenage leaders)
- Crutches (one crutch for every five teenage leaders)
- Wooden dowel rods or some equivalent (three rods for every five teenage leaders, approximately as long as their arms)
- Lots of ACE bandages and tape

This team builder requires some creativity on your part and a bit of preparation, but it's all worth it. Escort your teen leaders to a location that's a fair distance away from the church. (A half-mile away is good enough.) Have them sit down together as though they're seated on an airplane.

In great detail inform the kids that they were on a trip to a missionary project when their plane went down. The pilots were killed, along with several passengers, and the radio equipment was damaged in the crash. In short, they're stranded and have no way of contacting others. Do a good job when telling your story. This will help them understand why they can't use cell phones or just send somebody for help.

It gets worse. Not everybody survived the plane crash without injury. At this point have adult leaders walk around and assign injuries to certain kids within the group. Some will have broken arms. (These kids should have one dowel rod per kid wrapped to their arms so they *can't* use or bend them.) Others will have broken legs. (Disable one leg per kid as was done for the broken arms, but these kids should use crutches rather than dowel rods.) Some people in the group might have lost their vision. (Give each of these people a blindfold to wear.) Some sustained injuries to their mouths and can't speak. (A simple piece of tape across the lips of these kids will suffice.) Maybe a few are totally paralyzed. (Immobilize all four of their limbs.) Some will have no injury assigned to them. Use your imagination, but remember to leave a few leaders unhurt.

Now tell them that the objective is to get the *entire* group back to the church—in one trip. If you want, you can even assign a time limit. (If you have a really large group, you may want to divide them into a couple of smaller groups. And if your group is smaller, you can just keep them all together.)

CONTINUED ON NEXT PAGE

When you get back to the church, talk about the experience.

1. Ask some of the kids who were disabled, **What was it like to be injured?**
2. Ask everyone, **Were you able to contribute? If so, how?**
3. Ask everyone about the attitude of the group members: **How were people's attitudes on the way back?**
4. Ask a few what the activity taught them about teamwork.

NOTE: This might be difficult to pull off in a city environment. Some passersby may freak out if they see bandaged, blindfolded, and wounded teenagers hobbling down the sidewalk. So do this in an environment where you can pull off the team builder without any outside interruptions.

Also, make sure to have all of your necessary supplies located at the site of the crash so you can quickly get the kids into character.

LIGHT THE FIRE

It's probably clear that we need to be proactive about building and maintaining unity among our teenage leaders. As we conclude this chapter, we want to ask your permission to go old school for just a minute.

At the beginning of chapter 7, I joked about the good old-fashioned campfire where everyone gathered and sang "Kumbaya." As dated as that may sound, we'd like to tip our hats to the groups that made this practice popular many decades ago. Because as simple as it sounds, the "Kumbaya" campfire moments are as effective as they come when it comes to building unity.

A few years ago, I (Jonathan) led a fellowship group of young adults, and about 40 of us went on a weekend retreat. At the end of the retreat, we lit a nice big campfire, sang a little, and prayed a little, and then I opened the door for a time of sharing. I simply said, "Many of you have grown in the last year while being a part of this group. If you'd like to share what God has done in your life through this group, come, throw a stick in the fire, and share."

I had a pile of wood chopped really small so we had at least 40 small, dried sticks a few inches wide—small logs, really—that individuals could toss in the fire.

One by one people got up, tossed a stick in the fire, and shared what God had been doing in their lives and how the people sitting around the fire had helped. The more people shared, the deeper people got. Soon tears of joy started flowing, and the fire grew brighter and brighter.

Some of the tougher guys in the group began opening up, revealing layers of their lives that we'd never witnessed before. Walls broke down.

Hugs.

More sticks on the fire.

More tears.

All the while, the fire was getting bigger and bigger.

The fire grew so large, in fact, that the ranger came by and made us put it out! (True story. And it was a shame. It was an amazing fire!)

Those of us who were a part of that group still look back and laugh about that fire. But we also recognize the bonding that happened that night because it was pivotal for the group. In the years that this group was together, it was probably *the* defining moment that anyone in that group would name as the time they felt closest to the rest of the group.

Don't neglect the task of building and maintaining unity.

Teach unity.

Practice unity.

Re-create successful unity-building moments.

Equip teens to own the group's unity.

Consistently do team-building activities.

Who knows . . . maybe even sing "Kumbaya."

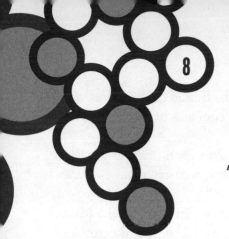

MINISTRY MAINTENANCE
WHAT DO YOU DO WHEN THAT "NEW MINISTRY SMELL" FADES AWAY?

Have you ever owned a new car? Everything about it is fresh, exciting, and fun.

A few years ago I (Jonathan) bought a brand-new Nissan Sentra. I know, I know—nothing fancy. But hey, I'm a youth worker. Whaddya expect? I was just thrilled to *finally* own a new car.

For the last two decades, I'd inherited other people's problem cars. When one of those problems finally went to "car heaven," we knew it was time for another car. So we began looking at used vehicles once again. When a friend of mine who owned a dealership learned we were looking for cars, he gave us an offer we couldn't refuse. Next thing we knew, we were driving a brand-new Nissan Sentra.

Ahhh . . . the smell! I love that new-car smell.

The seats! No cereal smashed into the creases.

The paint! No chips or dings—anywhere!

I didn't care that it was just a cheap little four-cylinder; it was new, and we loved it. If you've ever owned a new car, you know the feeling. Everyone loves a new car. And when you have one, you invent reasons to drive it. "Honey, I'll handle the carpool this morning." "Do you want me to go grocery shopping this week, sweetpea?" "No worries, sugar bear. I'll drop off Grandma at your parents' place . . . *in Idaho.*"

Now fast-forward 3,000 miles to the first service date. It's time for an oil change and a tune-up. And if you drive like my friend David, then you've probably already got a few dings in the door. What's worse is—the new-car smell is gone. In other words, what was once shiny and new isn't so shiny and new anymore, and now it's making some demands on you. And this is just the *first* service checkup; you'll need to do it all over again in another three months or so.

Of course, all car owners have the option of just skipping the regularly scheduled maintenance procedures on their car. They don't *have to* change the oil or filters. They don't *have to* inspect the brakes and tires. They don't *have to* check the fluids. But no car manufacturer or mechanic would recommend doing that. They know that as cool as a new car is, it still requires regular maintenance.

Does this remind you of ministry? Just as it is with new cars, new ministries are fun and exciting. But very soon you'll notice that the once brand-new ministry requires some ongoing attention to keep it from going to "ministry heaven."

A new teen leadership venture can be as fun as a new car. It's exciting to build a team of kids who lead and serve. But what happens a few months into it? Unless you maintain what you've built, it'll start sputtering and smoking.

You may have heard it said, "It's fun to catch fish but no fun to clean them."

"It's fun to catch fish but no fun to clean them."

Let's face it—maintenance isn't fun. Unlike the building phase when kids were excited, the ministry was growing, and teams produced disciples for Jesus, we rarely see any yield during the maintenance stage. Maintenance is one of those details that isn't urgent, so it gets shoved to the bottom of our to-do list and accomplished inconsistently. Then, to make matter worse, we rationalize it and say, "Oh, it's not really important."

Don't do this—don't dismiss the importance of maintenance.

Let's be honest with ourselves for a moment. (If you're a senior pastor reading this book, skip over this part, please.) Most youth workers are better builders than maintainers. That's just our nature. Many of us enjoy starting something new more than we enjoy maintaining something old. And that's fine. But it's not okay for us to totally neglect the maintenance side of things.

You've got to protect what you've built. Call it maintenance. Call it management. Whatever. Unless you focus some effort on "gassing up the ministry" or "checking the leadership's oil," it will eventually grind to a halt or, at the very least, be far less effective than you intended.

With that truth in mind, let's spend a short chapter talking about some of the most basic steps of maintenance that you should perform on your leadership program and the kids in it. We'll keep it short because if you've done the things we've outlined in the other chapters, then you're well on your way to maintaining a strong teen leadership ministry. Here are just a few more tidbits that will keep everything well-lubricated.

COMMUNICATE, COMMUNICATE, AND THEN COMMUNICATE SOME MORE

Communication is something we take for granted when we're on the giving end, so let's remind ourselves how important communication is if we're on the receiving end.

- You're married or engaged, and your significant other is on a long flight home from a trip overseas. How badly do you want to hear from your sweetie when that plane lands safely in the United States?
- Your child is sick. You've called the doctor and are now playing the waiting game. With every passing moment, you grow more anxious as you wait to hear what the pediatrician has to say.
- You're a solider behind enemy lines, and an air strike has been called in close to your position. Now you're waiting and hoping the coordinates that were sent to those pilots were *very* accurate.

Nobody likes to wait too long to receive important information. And nobody likes getting inaccurate information. Your kids won't, either.

I've never met a youth pastor who said, "You know, I really like making phone calls! I live for sending out the monthly calendar! When I wake up in the morning, the first thing on my mind is replying to all of the emails in my inbox!"

But all of those duties are important to the teens (and adults) who are walking beside you in the teen leadership ministry. Let me tell you just how important it is.

A couple of years ago, I (David) left behind 14 years of in-church youth ministry to join Jonathan and the team at The Source for Youth Ministry, where I focused all of my efforts on speaking, teaching, training, and developing resources for youth workers. It was a big change for me, and it was a big change for my church.

Before I vacated my position as the director of youth ministries, I sat down with some trusted leaders and friends and asked them to be brutally honest with me about my past leadership of them. I wanted to know what I'd done that was a blessing to them, and I also wanted to know about the things I'd goofed up.

One of the most interesting things that surfaced during these conversations with leaders—both kids and adults—was their desire for more communication on my part. I was a little surprised by this. After all, I sent weekly emails to my leaders describing the outreach and spiritual growth programs in detail, I made phone calls *daily*, I met with leaders twice a week, I mailed out a monthly calendar booklet, I kept the bulletin boards updated, and so on.

Without being defensive—*because I'd asked them for this feedback*—I repeated this litany of communication practices. They affirmed how much they'd appreciated what I'd done, but they still said it would've been nice to have *even more*. I was blown away—in a good way.

So many youth workers may think they're bothering their teens and adults with emails, phone calls, updates, and calendars. But if their team members are anything like mine were, then all of that communication is greatly appreciated and they'll probably welcome even more. And I don't want to meddle too much here . . . but some youth workers don't return calls or emails at all. Not only is this unprofessional, but it also tears down your ability to lead.

Keep the communication channels open.

So much needs to be communicated to our teen leaders: Meeting times, expectations, priorities, goals, and so on. On top of that, it's not always easy to communicate with a teenager, period. The best way to do it is to use whatever means he prefers—and often. If he likes talking on the phone, give him a call. If he likes talking in person, praise God and do that with him. If he likes texting, well—teens do like to text, but try to get them talking, too. Communicate, communicate, communicate!

We also need to learn to give feedback. A good rule in personnel management is, "Everybody wants to know the answer to, 'How am I doing?' even if they don't ask the question." Everyone from paid employees to volunteers wants to know whether they're performing well or poorly. So it's our job to let our teen leaders know how they're doing *and often*. We should *never* miss an opportunity to offer a word of encouragement to our leaders when they do a great job. Likewise, we should *never* miss an opportunity to talk with them lovingly about why a goal wasn't met.

None of our kids wants to fail; but from time to time, we all miss the mark. If you think you know why a leader suffered a setback, then jump in with her and offer some suggestions for solving the problem in the future. But whatever you do, *don't* wait to be asked for feedback. As tactfully as you can, give it often.

And since we're talking about genuine communication and not a one-way street, don't forget to *receive* feedback from your teen leaders—especially the ones you work with most closely in ministry. Routinely ask questions about good meeting times in order to stay current with their schedules. Ask a teen leader's opinion on how a project went. And be brave enough to ask teen leaders how they think you're doing.

We don't have to act on all of the feedback we receive from our teen leaders, but we do need to show them that we care about their thoughts and want to talk with them. Who knows? Maybe they'll have ideas that *will* shift how we do something. We won't know if we aren't secure enough to ask.

DEAL WITH PROBLEMS QUICKLY AND GENTLY

I don't believe that any of us are naive enough to think we'll have zero problems with our teenage leadership teams down the road. I mean, even those Type A people who change their oil every 3,000 miles on the dot still have to deal with the occasional dead battery or flat tire.

Therefore, you'll want to formalize a game plan for dealing with problems on the front end—*before* you face your first one. And whatever tactics you devise need to be communicated to all of the leaders, of course. Our chapter about avoiding pitfalls (chapter 9) goes into much more detail about handling specific problems that tend to be associated with teen leadership ministry. But some overarching strategies can be applied to a host of situations that you'll encounter, such as—

- What do we do if a teen leader is routinely absent from leadership meetings?
- Do we have a system in place for dealing with a kid who suffers a moral failure?
- How should we respond if a teen is doing a great job in our ministry, but we keep getting terrible reports about him from home or school?
- Who will address broken promises and dropped commitments, and how will they do it?
- What action should we take if we find a kid is mismatched with a ministry role?
- What should you do if Jeff keeps taking all of the pepperoni off your slices of pizza?

As you can see, some problems are more difficult than others.

While there aren't always easy solutions to these kinds of problems, we'll be wise to handle them quickly and gently. We can't jump in on only the big stuff that our teen leaders mess up; we must lovingly address each incident—even the little things. By doing so, we'll give the kids constant direction, which will hopefully prevent them from messing up big stuff in the future and keep them open to feedback.

We must be careful not to make mountains out of molehills. And likewise, we can't let a molehill *become* a mountain! Having a close relationship with our teen leaders, giving careful observations concerning their leadership and service, and communicating often will reduce a large number of potential problems. For those issues that do arise, we'll handle them quickly and gently.

By this time we'll have invested too much into these teen leaders just to lose them over junk we could have helped them to avoid. Let's do all we can to manage our teen leaders in such a way that they propel our ministry forward and, upon graduation from high school, proceed to the next chapter in their lives of service to God and God's kingdom.

KEEP MORALE HIGH

After reading that subhead, somewhere somebody just said, "Duh!" *I can feel it*.

Just ask anybody who knows me (David), and they'll tell you that I can usually be counted on to state the obvious.

But this one needed to be said—not because any youth worker is secretly planning ways to undermine her team of teen leaders and make them as miserable as humanly possible, but because we tend to notice morale only when it begins to slip.

But how do you keep morale high?

WIN—A LOT!

Maybe I'm a bit of a nerd, but I really love to study military history. (I probably get that from my grandfather who fought in World War II. And I'm constantly reading books, watching the History Channel, or looking for people in my community to talk with about their role in military campaigns.) In my unofficial research, I've concluded that low morale is usually a by-product of losing. Not too many successful brigades sat around moaning about the cold weather. On the flip side, those platoons who are in a stalemate with their enemies—or worse, getting beaten by them—are usually the ones who complain about everything.

The bottom line is this: Winning matters. If you're winning, it can cover up or at least greatly reduce many of the distractions that tend to cause low morale. So win as often and as big as you possibly can.

We know what winning looks like on a battlefield or in a baseball game, but what does winning look like in teenage leadership? Here are just a few of the observations you'll make about your teenage leadership ministry when it's winning:

- Teens are being led to Jesus for salvation and beginning to lead genuinely transformed lives. Perhaps this is because the outreach squad has engaged non-churched teens on campus and the small group leaders have invested time into them for the sake of the gospel. Regardless, you'll know your teenage leadership ministry is winning when it's winning souls.
- Teen leadership teams are continually growing in number (because of all those new believers) and in quality (because teens are understanding the importance of their leadership). You may have started off with just three teen leaders, but within a year, you now have five.
- The kids (and adults) in your ministry love one another deeply. Nope, you can't measure love; but you can tell whether or not you have it. When leaders were winning in the book of Acts, the believers grew not only in number, but also in love for one another. They spent time together, worshipped together, ate together, and even

shared their possessions with one another. They loved each other and it showed. If your leaders love one another, it'll be just as clear today as it was 2,000 years ago.

CELEBRATE—A LOT!

If you're winning, then new kids are being attracted to the ministry, teenagers are giving their lives to Jesus, personal transformations are constantly happening, and cool stories of God moments are springing up out of the lives of your kids. Gather everyone together and party!

That's right. I just prescribed a party.

Think about it: Most (profitable) companies in the business world host celebrations when major clients are won or big deals are brokered. Some even hand out bonus checks. Since you can't do the latter, opt instead to cater a meal, hand out a funny-looking trophy or prize, or throw an ice-cream party as a way of reveling in God's accomplishments.

Hey, this is biblical, people!

Even Jesus taught that when the kingdom of God wins, all of heaven celebrates. Check out what he says in Luke:

Then Jesus told them this parable: "Suppose one of you has a hundred sheep and loses one of them. Doesn't he leave the ninety-nine in the open country and go after the lost sheep until he finds it? And when he finds it, he joyfully puts it on his shoulders and goes home. Then he calls his friends and neighbors together and says, 'Rejoice with me; I have found my lost sheep.' I tell you that in the same way there will be more rejoicing in heaven over one sinner who repents than over ninety-nine righteous persons who don't need to repent.

"Or suppose a woman has ten silver coins and loses one. Doesn't she light a lamp, sweep the house and search carefully until she finds it? And when she finds it, she calls her friends and neighbors together and says, 'Rejoice with me; I have found my lost coin.' In the same way, I tell you, there is rejoicing in the presence of the angels of God over one sinner who repents." (15:3–10)

Knowing that heaven takes the time to party should cause us to build a little celebration into our own schedules.

ONE WORD: PERKS!

Another thing that all good business leaders know is that money isn't a motivator. Yeah, it certainly helps—but it's not what excites the heart. However, throwing your kids a few non-monetary perks every now and then will not only enhance your relationship with them but also supercharge your teen leadership ministry.

For years now my friends at Student Leadership University have hosted a *totally free* day of training that includes food, concerts, and an afternoon in the park at Universal Studios for youth workers and their teams. Since Orlando is an hour away from my church and home, I (David) have always taken full advantage of this fantastic offer.

When I've taken some of my older teen leaders, they always tell me how much fun they had, how much they learned, how they're going to be different, and how much they appreciated my thinking of them and extending an invitation to them. (It doesn't hurt that they got to skip a day of school, either.)

Seriously, the good news is, you don't have to rent out a theme park to throw your kids some well-deserved love. You can just show up at school one day with a pizza and wings and say thanks by saving a hardworking kid from eating yet another school lunch. If you live in a city that has a professional sports team (or three), you can call up the marketing reps, share a few stories about your impact on teenagers' lives, and ask them for some complimentary tickets. I've found them to be pretty generous when it's for a good cause.

The beauty of a perk is simple: It's not promised. So when kids get perks, they usually get amped up. And that's good for your teen leadership morale.

INTENTIONALLY ENCOURAGE YOUR TEEN LEADERS

I think that same reader just said, "Duh!" again.

Oh well.

Ministry usually keeps even the best leaders very busy. Just keeping the teen leadership machine running strong and in the right direction is more than a full-time job. Thus, it's easy to overlook the practice of intentionally encouraging your kids. But that's a terrible mistake to make—especially when encouraging them is so easy (and rewarding) to do.

Some of the best ways to lovingly encourage your teen leaders are sending them notes, shooting them heartfelt texts, or leaving them appreciative voice mails on their home answering machines (where their parents can hear them, too). You can also just show up in person and tell them thanks. Regardless of how you do it, do it.

I can't tell you how many times I've been visiting with kids at their homes, and their parents have shown me where one of my personal notes—that I gave to their child a month ago—is hanging on the fridge. Or a teen will scramble off to his room and return with a quick letter that I scribbled to him a year earlier.

That sort of stuff matters to kids.

And why wouldn't it? Like celebrating, this is biblical stuff.

Think about Paul's many letters to the early churches spread across Asia Minor. Today, many of us turn to the New Testament letters for doctrinal truth, church leadership strategies, or even early church history. But these ancient manuscripts served an important—

although much lighter—purpose when they were originally written two millennia ago. When people read Paul's letters, they were usually encouraged.

Paul often sought to fortify and inspire his newfound family and friends. Check out a few of these lines from several of his letters.

Romans 1:7–12 reads—

To all in Rome who are loved by God and called to be his holy people:

Grace and peace to you from God our Father and from the Lord Jesus Christ.

First, I thank my God through Jesus Christ for all of you, because your faith is being reported all over the world. God, whom I serve in my spirit in preaching the gospel of his Son, is my witness how constantly I remember you in my prayers at all times; and I pray that now at last by God's will the way may be opened for me to come to you.

I long to see you so that I may impart to you some spiritual gift to make you strong—that is, that you and I may be mutually encouraged by each other's faith.

In his thankful letter to the church at Philippi, Paul sent these words:

Grace and peace to you from God our Father and the Lord Jesus Christ.

I thank my God every time I remember you. In all my prayers for all of you, I always pray with joy because of your partnership in the gospel from the first day until now, being confident of this, that he who began a good work in you will carry it on to completion until the day of Christ Jesus.

It is right for me to feel this way about all of you, since I have you in my heart and, whether I am in chains or defending and confirming the gospel, all of you share in God's grace with me. God can testify how I long for all of you with the affection of Christ Jesus.

And this is my prayer: that your love may abound more and more in knowledge and depth of insight, so that you may be able to discern what is best and may be pure and blameless for the day of Christ, filled with the fruit of righteousness that comes through Jesus Christ—to the glory and praise of God. (Philippians 1:2–11)

One more example should settle the point. Consider these heartfelt words to Timothy, Paul's son and partner in the faith:

To Timothy, my dear son:

Grace, mercy and peace from God the Father and Christ Jesus our Lord.

I thank God, whom I serve, as my ancestors did, with a clear conscience, as night and day I constantly remember you in my prayers. Recalling your tears, I long to see you, so that I may be filled with joy. I am reminded of your sincere faith, which first lived in your grandmother Lois and in your mother Eunice and, I am persuaded, now lives in you also.

For this reason I remind you to fan into flame the gift of God, which is in you through the laying on of my hands. For the Spirit God gave us does not make us timid, but gives us power, love and self-discipline. (2 Timothy 1:2–7)

Do you see a common theme? Paul knew he had to encourage his leaders if he didn't want them to fail in the face of withering persecution, desperate temptation, or worse—hypocrisy. Take a page from Paul's playbook and encourage your teen leaders.

All of these simple strategies will go a long way toward maintaining high morale on your team. Invest a little creative time into devising some more ways to show your leaders some love. You'll be glad you did.

PREVENTIVE MAINTENANCE

Strong communication, appropriate responses to problems, and a careful eye on morale will help ensure that your teenage leadership ministry fires on all eight cylinders. There are other preventive maintenance steps you can take as well. But I promised you a short chapter, so I need to wrap this up pretty soon.

One of the most helpful procedures you can perform is to ask yourself if *you'd* be fulfilled as a teen leader if you were involved in this ministry. Just continually ask yourself some tough questions:

- Am I truly empowering my kids for ministry, or am I just delegating work to them?
- As the point person for the ministry, am I functioning at my best for the sake of those who are leading with me?
- Are ongoing and honest evaluations of the teenage leadership ministry being performed?
- Are any adaptations necessary? If so, what are they, and how do we incorporate them?

The importance of performing maintenance on your teenage leadership ministry can't be overstated. I'd be lying if I said it was always easy or always fun. But the truth is, maintenance on your ministry often boils down to "pay me now or pay me later." Everyone knows it's far easier—and cheaper—to prevent problems than to fix them. So make sure you schedule the necessary time to keep your teen leadership ministry running strong.

The good news is, you only have to maintain your teenage leadership for as long as you want to have it. Performing regular maintenance tasks is the closest you'll come to having an insurance policy for the leadership ministry you've worked so hard to build. If you take maintenance seriously—doing it often and in detail—you can expect to get lots of mileage out of your teen leaders.

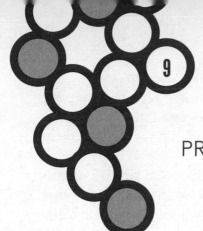

SIDESTEPPING PITFALLS
PRACTICAL WAYS TO AVOID THE SNARES OF TEENAGE LEADERSHIP

Since I'm a child of the '80s, I (David) was exposed to a rather iconic—and unique—action hero. He couldn't shoot laser beams from his eyes, nor was he bulletproof; but he had his fair share of world-saving attributes.

He was intellectual *and* suave—*at the same time*. He modeled grit and fierce determination whether he was staring down evil Nazis (again) or caught in a temple of doom. Nobody else in Hollywood had a theme song as recognizable as his. And unlike other heroes who wore brightly colored, skintight spandex and ridiculous capes, this dude wore a brown leather jacket and one supercool hat.

Of course I'm talking about everybody's favorite pistol-toting, whip-cracking archaeologist—Indiana Jones.

As a kid I couldn't get enough of this guy! I mean, who else flew airplanes, drove tanks, solved ancient riddles, fought in sword duels, stared Hitler in the face—and lived to tell about it?

At one point or another, every boy I knew *who was worth his salt* attempted to swing off a ledge or over a ditch while hanging on to the end of a rope that had been fashioned into a makeshift whip. We all wanted to be like Indy.

Life was never a cakewalk for Indiana Jones. When he set out on an adventure, he always had plenty of questions: *Will I recover the artifact? Does X mark the spot? Can the Nazis truly be stopped? Will I get the girl this time?*

Yet in spite of all these unknowns, Indy could always count on one certainty—plenty of pitfalls. In one scene he might be thrashing around in a pit of vipers, and later on he could very well find himself trapped in a subterranean tunnel system with the walls closing in on him.

You're also embarking on a pitfall-laden adventure. If you've tried implementing a teenage leadership ministry before—heck, if you've even *thought* about starting a teenage leadership ministry—then you know there are pitfalls just waiting to ensnare you and your efforts. But unlike the fictitious pitfalls that Indiana Jones faced, the ones in your world can seriously jeopardize your plans for a teen leadership ministry—or derail them altogether.

Like Indy, we must learn how to sidestep the various hazards that could keep our dreams from becoming a reality. This chapter will identify some of the most insidious pitfalls that can halt your teen leadership plans and, more importantly, give you a few practical strategies for bypassing or overcoming them.

This isn't an exhaustive list. Unfortunately, teens can encounter more pitfalls than we can list here. But these are some of the worst—in no particular order—that you'll want to avoid like poisoned darts shot from the spider-web-infested wall of an ancient tomb.

CLIQUES

Whether or not they have a teen leadership program, every youth leader I know complains about cliques in their ministries. They speak of the impenetrable walls their kids build around sports, music, interests, and anything else they can conjure up from the various subcultures that exist today. And if a teenager doesn't hold to a certain like or dislike that's congruent with the group, then that teen isn't welcome.

It's fairly easy to see how cliques can develop in a youth ministry that employs kids as leaders. Think about it: A core group of teens bands together, is trained to function in a very specific role, works hard, and spends their off time with each other building stronger relationships. None of this is bad, but all of it has the potential to create cliques. On the one hand, you want to develop synergy among the team members, as well as a deep sense of fellowship. But on the other hand, you want all of your teen leaders to be open to acclimating new kids into the ministry and its leadership teams.

Today's New Testament has been translated into English from the original Greek. And the Greek language uses an interesting word to describe the fellowship, community, and overall intimacy that the early church had with one another: *Koinonia*. This word accurately describes the desperately close relationship that early believers had with Jesus and one another. It's best seen in Acts 2:42–47.

> They devoted themselves to the apostles' teaching and to fellowship, to the breaking of bread and to prayer. Everyone was filled with awe at the many wonders and signs performed by the apostles. All the believers were together and had everything in common. They sold property and possessions to give to anyone who had need. Every day they continued to meet together in the temple courts. They broke bread in their homes and ate together with glad and sincere hearts, praising God and enjoying the favor of all the people. And the Lord added to their number daily those who were being saved.

According to this passage, these people did *life*—not just ministry—together. Look at the text again. They worshipped together, sold property to assist others financially, met in homes to share meals with one another—and as a result, God blessed them. God knew these believers could be trusted with other people, so God added to their number daily.

It's not always easy to see cliques developing, but they're usually pretty obvious once they've formed. Here's when you know your teen leadership teams have crossed the line from *koinonia* to clique:

- They don't love others (even if they say they do).
- They place restrictions on new members that weren't placed on themselves.
- They're unwilling to help train new members.
- They commit group sins, such as gossip or jealousy.
- They're verbally or physically hesitant to add other leaders to "their" team.

Cliques are inward focused. *Koinonia* is outward focused. *Cliques* never allow God to add to their numbers. *Koinonia* is contagious.

You can eliminate a large portion of the headache that comes with cliques by asking your teen leaders to be on the lookout for new and upcoming leaders.

> # You can eliminate a large portion of the headache that comes with cliques by asking your teen leaders to be on the lookout for new and upcoming leaders.

Yep, get them thinking beyond themselves from the start. Teen leaders can be tasked with not only finding other teen leaders, but also assisting in their training and development.

You might want to ask cliquish teen leaders some hard questions about their mind-set and actions, such as—"What eventually happens to our ministry if we don't add others to the team?" and, "Is there a good reason for depriving someone of the excitement and meaning you've found by serving in our ministry?" This should help them come around to the idea of new kids being added to the leadership roster.

PRIDE

Steven was one of the best guitar players I (David) have ever had the opportunity to plug into a teen worship band. This kid was scary good and remains so to this day as he studies to become a full-time ministry leader. But once upon a time, Steven faced a tremendous struggle with pride.

Steven was a part of that worship band I mentioned a few chapters ago—the one that had to learn a hard lesson on top of Mount Pumpkin. Steven was our lead guitarist, and at times he acted as though the success of the entire team rose and fell with his ability. He played such hot licks up on the stage that the excited crowd would chant his name—even though they should've been worshipping Jesus.

It reached a climax one evening as Steven stepped toward the front of the stage, brought the guitar up to his face, and began playing with his teeth—just like Jimi Hendrix did decades ago. The crowd loved it. I hated it.

Like all of our worship leaders, Steven knew there was a huge difference between rocking a concert and leading praise to God. During a concert, bands are basically saying, "Look at me! Bow to me!" But worship bands are saying, "Look at God! Bow to God!" Steven's dental maneuver would've been fine at a concert (although personally, I can recommend better tools for flossing); but it was completely inappropriate during worship.

I knew I had to address the problem immediately, but I wondered what a suitable response looked like. Knowing that Jimi also set guitars on fire and smashed them, I considered doing both to Steven. But eventually I dismissed that idea as more Neanderthal than pastoral.

I privately reprimanded Steven for his onstage antics that totally undermined the purpose for the evening. At first Steven rejected my input because, after all, I was battling his pride, and pride never likes to be threatened. But in the end our talk did help solve the problem; Steven stepped back in line and helped lead the band from a godlier and more humble standpoint.

Pride is one of the sneakiest sins that ministry leaders face, whether it's within us or within our kids. We want to be good at ministry, so we work hard to become so. We train, we study, we practice, and then *we do*. Eventually, the effectiveness we've sought after comes to fruition. And then a strange thing happens: We tend to become prideful or arrogant about our success or effectiveness (which God has granted to us).

Usually then, in some way or another, we become conscious of our prideful condition and seek to change our hearts about this personal shortcoming. Here's where pride can get really funky, though. One possible response is modeling false humility. We verbally repel compliments while silently agreeing with (and relishing) everything positive that's said about us.

Another temptation comes from putting our pride in check only to become proud of our humility. One youth worker once said, "I'm the best at being humble."

Right back to square one.

Perhaps it's because of pride's nature that God tells us so often in the Bible how much he despises pride. The Bible even gives us a specific warning in Proverbs 16:18, "Pride goes before destruction, a haughty spirit before a fall."

Pride is often a "gateway sin," meaning it can lead to other problems that may be even worse. For example, pride can easily lead to a sense of religious superiority. This characterized most of the Pharisees from Jesus' day. They believed they were holier than other people, when in fact Jesus confronted them on the most elementary of faith values.

When pride sets in, it can also lead to an attitude of judgment or condemnation toward others. We've seen this displayed on the news networks at times. One so-called Christian group blasts another one because the first group views any lifestyle or belief that's not their own as being inferior. Pride can also affect us as individuals when it happens in our own ministry settings. One kid isolates himself from the others because he thinks he's more devout than the rest.

One of the best ways to help kids overcome pride is by continually reminding teen leaders that they're servants first. Like Jesus, our teen leaders must be willing to serve others. Remember, the first part of our leadership training isn't teaching kids how to lead Bible studies—but how to be like Jesus. If you maintain that stance from the beginning, it's easier to help your leaders avoid pride down the line.

Bear in mind that the more high-profile a teen leader is, the more likely she is to face pride. You probably won't notice too much arrogance among those who help you with office duties, but you may have to deal with it more often than you want to with the kids in the worship band or on the drama team, or even your small group leaders.

If you find this to be the case, just make sure you're offering those same kids opportunities to serve outside the spotlight. In other words, put them in situations where they're not on the stage, behind the microphone, or in command of the small group. You might—

- ask the Drama team to set up chairs for the kids who will watch their next sketch;
- invite the Worship team to clean the stage and sound area regularly; or
- have the small group leaders sweep the floors.

Another pride-prevention tactic is to ask your teen leaders to help govern themselves. That's right. Put your kids on "personal pride patrol." Pride can't hide itself; that's against its nature. So ask your teen leaders to be on guard against pride in their own lives and in the lives of their peers. And if (or when) they spot pride, instruct them to address it quickly and gently.

I've noticed the positive influence that one kid's critique can have on another kid—if it's given from a loving standpoint. Something you and I have to address with a teenager over and over again can be handled in one conversation if it happens between peers. Don't forget to tap into this resource at your disposal.

Further, warn the youth about the sinister nature of pride. Help them understand that pride alone is damaging enough, but it usually brings with it even more devastation. Help them learn how to guard their hearts against pride. The possible outcomes of pride are far too severe to be tolerated in your teenage leadership ministry.

LACK OF TEAMWORK

The need to build and maintain unity is so great that we already devoted an entire chapter in this book to it (chapter 7). However, a lack of teamwork is such an important topic that we felt it necessary to list it as one of the pitfalls within this chapter, too.

The problems associated with a lack of teamwork stem partly from the fact that this can be a two-headed monster at times. As we've already said, teamwork must be maintained not only on each team (among individual teens), but also among the various teams (for instance, the Kitchen team and the Missions team). This isn't an easy task, and it usually requires as much attention as watching out for the development of pride.

So many things can upset the harmony on a particular teen leadership team. One kid could become prideful; another could become lazy. One could receive more credit than others for the work accomplished. Or the problems could exist between various teams. The Greeter team could become jealous of the fact that the Drama team always gets to be up front. The Worship team could fall into an argument with the Tech team over what the music should sound like. In short, any number of difficulties could derail the unity you work so hard to protect.

This isn't to say all conflict is bad. Conflict is a way of life. Part of our roles as mentors or adult leaders is to help our youth learn how to deal with conflict in a positive way. Unfortunately, out-of-control conflict withers the unity you've built.

Even Jesus faced a lack of teamwork in his ministry:

Then James and John, the sons of Zebedee, came to him. "Teacher," they said, "we want you to do for us whatever we ask."

"What do you want me to do for you?" he asked.

They replied, "Let one of us sit at your right and the other at your left in your glory."

"You don't know what you are asking," Jesus said. "Can you drink the cup I drink or be baptized with the baptism I am baptized with?"

"We can," they answered.

Jesus said to them, "You will drink the cup I drink and be baptized with the baptism I am baptized with, but to sit at my right or left is not for me to grant. These places belong to those for whom they have been prepared."

When the ten heard about this, they became indignant with James and John. Jesus called them together and said, "You know that those who are regarded as rulers of the Gentiles lord it over them, and their high officials exercise authority over them. Not so with you. Instead, whoever wants to become great among you must be your servant, and whoever wants to be first must be slave of all. For even the Son of Man did not come to be served, but to serve, and to give his life as a ransom for many." (Mark 10:35–45)

For whatever reason, James and John felt as though they deserved more and better of Jesus when eternity finally rolled around. Jesus didn't cave in and give them what they requested; instead, he gave them a lesson on seeking not authority but servanthood. He even submitted himself to this standard, reminding them that he'd come to serve and give his life for the sake of others. Jesus knew he couldn't afford division within his group of disciples.

In fact, Jesus emphasized unity and teamwork in his teaching ministry. On at least one occasion, Jesus took time to teach about division. When he was accused of being empowered by a demonic force, Jesus slyly responded in Mark 3:23–26 by saying, "How can Satan drive out Satan? If a kingdom is divided against itself, that kingdom cannot stand. If a house is divided against itself, that house cannot stand. And if Satan opposes himself and is divided, he cannot stand; his end has come."

If you're like Jesus, you may have a catchy little parable up your sleeve to help you deal with moments of disharmony. That's great! But if not, rest assured there are some highly practical things you can do with your team members to help synergize them:

1. *Teach about the body of Christ (as in the* one and only *body of Christ).* No matter how many teen leaders or leadership teams you have, you still have only one youth ministry. You can pull scriptural evidence of this idea straight from the apostle Paul's teaching in 1 Corinthians 12, where he talks about one body having many parts.

2. *Spend time together.* I always liked taking the worship band to a few Christian concerts each year—not to study stage presence, song transitions, or worship leading styles, but just to have a good time together. And it worked pretty well. It gave the hardworking worship leaders some quality downtime with one another and with me. You might take the Drama team to the performing arts studio in your area.

Your Greeter team could visit . . . okay, I'm not sure what kind of venue your greeters could visit. But the good news is you don't have to connect so many dots. Just invite kids to your house for some tacos and *Nacho Libre* (for the seventeenth time). Chances are good they won't appreciate the concert or plays or movie as much as they enjoy spending quality time with their friends and with you.

3. *Intentionally cultivate teamwork.* Make team-building activities a regular part of your training time. These give kids a chance to laugh, have fun together, bond a little more, and get used to working together to accomplish a task. We've included a bunch of our favorite team builders in chapter 7.

MORAL FAILURE

We mentioned earlier that each of these pitfalls should be avoided like the plague. That's true and we still mean it. But moral failure may be the single most devastating pitfall. When a teenage leader surrenders to a moral failure, the pain and expense can be extensive.

It was in Kyle's case.

Kyle was one of the most dedicated believers in my (David's) ministry. And he wasn't dedicated just to our ministry's programs, but also to Jesus. He always had his Bible with him—even at the lunch table in the high school cafeteria. He was usually the first one willing to lead whatever charge I put forth in the ministry. He loved the other kids in our ministry; he prayed with and for them both publically and privately. Kyle was so awesome that most of my teens probably thought Jesus loved him more than anyone else on the planet.

But Kyle struggled with an inner turmoil that ended up rocking his world one day. Though Kyle spent seven afternoons a week teaching Bible studies, leading small groups, helping in the children's ministry, and planning outreach events at the church, he also spent his evenings perusing online pornography sites.

Like all sin, it was eventually found out. I'll never forget answering his mother's phone call that Thursday afternoon and listening to her sob through the disappointment, frustration, and fear that had crashed into her world an hour earlier. Like all sin, it had consequences. Kyle was embarrassed and lost close friends over the matter. He decided it was best that he switch schools, which cost him even more close relationships. Since he was too embarrassed to come around the church anymore, he suffered the loss of his spiritual family as well. Further, all the ministry plates he'd been spinning dropped, which meant lots of other kids under his leadership suffered from the void that Kyle's sin created in their lives.

It was a tough day. The huge pain that our ministry felt—due to the nature of dealing with the sin (quelling rumors, asking for patience and privacy, and finding Kyle's replace-

SIDESTEPPING PITFALLS 127

ment)—was eclipsed only by the pain that his family faced. When a teen in whom you've invested so much forfeits his character for a moment or a month, you (the leader) tend to wear a little bit of that failure, too. It's unnecessary but understandable. You've invested so much into the kid, and he's broken your trust. If you aren't careful, you may find yourself doubting your abilities as the ministry leader because so much of your identity as a youth worker is wrapped up in your kids' progress.

Moral failure is one of the problems you want to *prevent*, not *fix*.

Moral failure is one of the problems you want to *prevent*, not *fix*.

Prevention takes a lot of effort, but it's worth every single moment you devote to it. You must understand that every one of your teen leaders who's serving the kingdom of God has a mark on her life from the Enemy—Satan. The Devil's strategy since Jesus' resurrection has been to destroy those who call themselves disciples through various forms of hypocrisy. Realize that the Devil will provide your beloved teen leaders with an unlimited number of opportunities for them to betray their personal commitment to Christ and your ministry.

Before you read any further, set down this book and think about how many ministry leaders (volunteer or paid, ordained or lay, adult or teen) you know who chose paths that cost them dearly. No, seriously, put it down. Go ahead.

Now, with those regretful stories in mind, let's plot a course that will help your current teen leaders avoid similar fates. The more tactics you have in your arsenal, the better.

For starters, teach on moral failure repeatedly. In fact, I suggest that at least once a month you talk directly to your teen leaders about what it means to be a Christlike servant leader, filled with integrity and character. There are plenty of illustrations you can use from the Bible to teach this truth. And you probably know other ministry leaders who've fallen short of a godly expectation; you could pull nuggets of usable wisdom from their stories (avoid using names, of course). Don't forget to talk about the scars you've accrued over the years from falling below the line of reproach. Whatever your approach, be frequent with it. Let your kids know you take this pitfall very seriously.

While no tactic guarantees total prevention of moral failure, one does stand head and shoulders above the rest: One-on-one discipleship. Yeah, we've already harped on it in preceding chapters, but one-on-one relationships focused on discipleship truly are the best line of defense against this specific pitfall. These relationships give you prime windows of opportunity in which to ask touchy questions and inject important lessons into your teen leaders' lives. Do all you can to take full advantage of these crucial relationships.

From a leadership and managerial standpoint, it's best to address small problems before they become big ones. For instance, if you notice one of your teen leaders has some rather risqué conversations with his girlfriend on his Facebook wall, you may decide to jump in before the situation escalates to sex (if it hasn't already). If you discover a teen leader of yours has been less than honest with one of her peers, your adult leaders, or yourself, then you should consider having a conversation with her about integrity. You want to do all you can to prevent *hiccups* from becoming *blowups*.

You want to do all you can to prevent *hiccups* from becoming *blowups*.

In general, be up front about the pain that moral failure can cause. Lovingly make kids aware of the consequences they'll face and the negative implications others will feel as a result of their actions. This isn't a time to use scare tactics or the "fire and brimstone" approach. Just give them the information they need to make decisions that honor God and their commitment to God.

No matter how hard you try to keep your kids free from this pitfall, some of your teen leaders may still experience moral failure. That's just the reality of sin, unfortunately.

In the case I mentioned above, Kyle removed himself from his leadership roles. However, it's not uncommon for some teenagers to want to remain in leadership in spite of their sin. How you handle that situation becomes very important.

You'll want to deal with it as quickly as accuracy allows. By that I mean you should take action as quickly as possible, but only after you've collected all of the pertinent facts, talked with the proper people, heard both sides of the story, and developed a plan for dealing with it. There's no sense in making a bad situation worse with incorrect information or untenable plans.

As tough as it may be, moral failure requires us to remove a kid from her leadership position. We can't permit someone who's allowed sin to reign in her life to continue influencing others.

I hadn't been in youth ministry for very long when I had to deal with this issue for the first time. When "Mike" chose immorality with his girlfriend, I asked my pastor for help. He gently but resolutely declared, "We have to love Mike enough to remove him from his position. If we let him stay where he is, we won't be loving him like we should."

But don't just kick a morally depraved teen to the curb. That's the *very last* thing she needs. When a teen experiences the pain and shame associated with moral failure, she may feel unlovable. Do everything in your power to show her your love. And make sure she hears you say, "I love you," as often as possible. Remind her that Jesus loves her as well.

Beyond that, you'll need to get your teen leader whatever form of help she requires. Maybe it's as simple as Bible study and prayer with another godly adult. Maybe it's an accountability partner. Maybe it's professional counseling. Whatever it is, move heaven and earth to ensure she gets the help she needs.

Finally, check on her regularly. You don't have to bug your kid, and you don't want to seem intrusive, but let her know she's one of your chief concerns until she regroups from her failure.

Work hard and pray harder that you never have to help a teen through moral failure. But be prepared to handle these kinds of situations with love and grace should they ever arise in your ministry.

COMPLACENCY

Nobody is immune to complacency, the apathetic and spiritless rut that negatively affects all that we do. No matter where we are in life or ministry, complacency can swoop in undetected and ruin hearts. As ministry leaders ourselves, we can isolate those moments of complacency in the areas of life that matter most to us: Our relationships with God, our marriages, our families, our dedication to NASCAR—whatever.

Most of us will admit to becoming complacent in our ministry at one time or another. At those times we're basically feeling bored with what God is doing in our ministry. Perhaps we've fallen into ruts. Maybe we're not seeing growth—numerical or spiritual. Or maybe our ministries are growing, but we had different ideas about what they'd look like by now.

Teenagers are no different. Truth be told, they're probably more susceptible to complacency than most. They can easily become bored with the latest and greatest in life. They see blockbuster after blockbuster at the movie theater; pump the latest tunes into their ears via their MP3 players; and visit a myriad of theme parks, concerts, shows, and sporting events. Knowing this, we have a daunting task to keep kids excited about serving God in our local church setting. How you handle their tendency toward complacency will dictate in large part the longevity of your ministry.

Never stop talking about how important the kids' ministry is. If they play in the band, follow up with visitors, or take care of the group's soda machine, remind them in genuine ways exactly how important they—and their work—are to the youth ministry. I say "genuine" because it's not necessary or helpful to invent false importance. Just tell them how grateful you, the church, and their peers are for their service.

As you talk with your teen leaders about ministry, continually show them unmet needs. We know ministry never ends, but they may not know that. Be careful not to overwhelm them, but stave off complacency by showing them what else needs to be done. For example, when a visitor gives her life to Jesus, celebrate that with your teams but then ask them to focus their efforts on helping her reach her non-church friends. Nothing combats complacency as well as new challenges do. In a careful and pastoral manner, apply incremental pressure to help keep your teen leaders sharp. Have faith that they can grow and handle more responsibility.

You might also try putting a face on the ministry. Our youth ministry made a fairly aggressive move one year and decided to adopt seven different children through Compassion International. I asked for the kids' approval first so it wouldn't be a surprise, and then I completed all of the paperwork and began the monthly process of collecting money. The plan was that each grade level would be responsible for funding a child around the world.

Within six months I noticed a drop-off in financial support for this important cause. I reminded the kids that they'd made a promise to God and to their Compassion children, but that did little in the way of bringing in the needed funds. We tinkered with the way we took the offering, but that also failed to bring in the money necessary to support the children.

Finally, I asked my assistant to hang up 8x10 glossy pictures of our Compassion International children around our youth building. She took it a step further and plastered smaller pictures of those kids' faces on a huge world map that she also put up on the wall. Finally, she made wallet-sized copies of the children's photos and gave each of our kids one photo to take home and place on their fridge.

Even though we set out to hang up a few pictures, what we actually did was put faces on the need. Once we did that, our teens snapped out of their complacency and resumed their giving. If you want to combat complacency, one simple way is to put a face on the need.

To ward off complacency, you can also focus on the number of wins your team has. Every time a goal is met—a visitor receives Jesus, a small group gets started, or an event goes according to plan—take the time to celebrate exactly what happened. Make sure to thank the kids for their roles in the win.

Everyone wants to be a part of something significant. However, it might not occur to your teen leaders that their roles in the ministry are actually significant. So it will be up to you to help them understand. Take the time to explain to them exactly how greeting, teaching, cooking, serving, or praying is significant. For example, if you can, tie a kid's decision to accept Jesus back to when he was first invited by the Campus Outreach team to attend the youth group. Remembering to celebrate these kinds of victories helps prevent complacency from setting in.

BUSY KIDS

If you're in youth ministry at any level—volunteer helper or full-time professional—you've noticed that today's kids are busy. They've got academic obligations hanging over them. They're trying to round out their college résumés with community service and extracurricular clubs. If they have lives outside of school, they usually involve sports practices, a part-time job—and (uh-oh!) significant others. Their calendars are as packed as Fortune 500 CEOs'.

Knowing that kids are so busy has caused some youth workers to omit them from leadership. That's a mistake. You can't overlook them—you just have to be careful when asking for their help. The pitfall of overly busy kids can be managed more easily if it's done on the front end. Not doing so may jeopardize your competence and trust in the eyes of the parents.

You must be honest about ministry expectations and obligations from the beginning of the application process. That's why it's so important to include a **My Commitment** form like the sample in chapter 4. Counsel with teenagers and parents about all of the expectations. For instance, if a talented and qualified teen wants to join the worship band, one of the best things to do is sit down and talk with her about all of the responsibilities that are involved in that role. Most kids think the band serves only once a week on the regularly scheduled youth ministry night. They don't think about the practices, the search for new material, the memorization of music, the investment of time for the sake of creativity, the sound checks, the setups, the teardowns, and so on. It's up to you to educate them about these expectations on the front end, before they get bogged down by all the work and ultimately disappoint themselves, you, and the ministry team.

One of the things parents are going to want to hear about is the time commitment. They'll want to know when practices or training sessions occur. They'll want to know how many nights each week or month are required. They'll want to know whether busy seasons in the school year will be taken into account. For all of these questions—and any others the parents come up with—you must be brutally honest. It's better to communicate clearly from the start than find yourself apologizing down the road.

When my little brother and I were younger, I would incessantly try to get him to help me with my chores by promising an unrealistically small time investment: "C'mon, Michael, let's go wash and wax my car. It'll take only 10 minutes." Or, "Hey, bro! Come help me mow the six-acre front yard. We'll be done in, like, half an hour." Well, my little brother quickly caught on to this scheme, and to this day he reminds me of it every chance he gets. Your teen leaders and their parents will also catch on if you're unrealistic or dishonest with them.

You may even want to run your teen leadership ministry in manageable chunks of time. Teenagers' lives happen in semesters. Take into consideration the times when midterms and final exams are happening. Plan training sessions and mission projects during downtimes in school schedules, such as the summer, Christmas vacation, or spring break. Also, don't burden your teen leaders with unnecessary meetings. If you can get away with monthly training sessions instead of weekly ones, opt for those—especially if you're meeting with teen leaders one-on-one.

These simple strategies will help keep your busy kids from becoming burned-out kids.

PITFALL PATROL

We've explored some of the biggest pitfalls you'll face in starting and managing a teen leadership program in your youth ministry. As I said earlier, this isn't an exhaustive list of pitfalls; these are simply some of the bigger ones.

You'll never be able to eliminate every pitfall from your kids' paths. And that means you'll always be on pitfall patrol. You have to keep a careful eye on potential problems. Regardless of which pitfalls you'll face, every single one of them requires intentionality in dealing with it.

Fortunately, a few simple habits will go a long way toward helping youth pastors avoid pitfalls:

1. *One-on-one discipleship.* (Hey, we warned you that you hadn't heard our last rant on the subject!) Seriously, if you're committed to supporting your teen leaders in these kinds of relationships, you'll spot problems a lot further out, be able to deal with them much more privately, and help them put boundaries in place that will steer them clear of future pitfalls.

2. *Regular training.* You, along with your trusted team of parents and adult volunteers, need to determine how often is considered "regular" for your teen leaders, but a good rule of thumb is monthly. That frequency typically avoids the burnout potential associated with weekly meetings, plus it gives teen leaders an adequate amount of time to take action on the lessons from the previous meeting. You and your adult mentors can call, text, and meet with your teen leaders face-to-face in between meetings, discussing what they've learned and challenging them to live it out day by day.

3. *Team-building activities.* These fun and engaging practices offer so much to your teen leaders. They allow teens to learn about one another, they teach them how to work more closely and effectively, and they give them much-needed opportunities to play together. Don't miss chapter 7 (if you've been skipping around in the book). It's completely dedicated to building unity on your team, and we share several of our most popular and impactful team builders in it.

Take pitfalls seriously and do all you can to spare your kids from falling into them.

REAL-LIFE MINISTRY BY TEENAGERS
TEENAGE LEADERSHIP IN MOTION

Teen leadership is nothing new. The fact is, healthy ministries have been developing teen leaders for decades. That means that as you're reading this chapter, teen leadership programs might already exist near you.

If you're like us, then you might want to see some examples of real-life teen leadership in action. We encourage you to contact other churches and ministries in your area and ask if they're developing teen leaders. If they're developing teams of kids doing ministry, stop by and take a peek. Glean some wisdom from the leaders of these ministries, learn from their experiences, and ask for their perspective on what works and what doesn't.

We're always amazed by how much we learn from just watching another ministry in action.

At the same time, we realize that your time might be limited and you might not be able to devote hours upon hours to visiting other ministries. With that in mind, this chapter takes you on a global journey to look at 10 different ministries that are developing teenage leaders around the world. These simple examples will give you a snapshot of real-life teen leadership.

LIVING EXAMPLES

Below you'll find 10 real-life examples of ministry by kids. First, you'll read the living examples as described by the adult who's in charge of each ministry. Then you'll see *our take* on what's described. Enjoy!

Right now we're hosting monthly Draft Experiences (Draft XP), where we take our group of 35 teen leaders to a unique environment to hear from Christian leaders within our community. We keep these experiences a mystery until the kids are on site. So far we've taken them to a bank downtown—we took them into the vault and server rooms to have the bank president talk to them about the importance of integrity, security, and trust. We took them to a football team's locker room to hear a local high school coach talk with them about impacting lives and teamwork. We've also had them meet at local eateries that everyone loves and led them in discussions about loyalty, service, and so on.

So our development piece is once a month and it's *always* off the church campus because we want the kids to also serve on ministry teams within our church and in local parachurch and service organizations.

After our Draft XP, we meet one-on-one with each teen to discuss his passions and gifts and then help him connect the dots between what he's passionate about and any local or church opportunities. This program has greatly increased teen ownership within our church and teen ministry.

—JARM TURNER

OUR TAKE: Jarm is really capitalizing on experiential learning and mentoring. We love how he switches it up each month and takes his kids off-site to train them. It's a safe bet his kids are more keyed in to these types of training sessions than they would be if they were just sitting in the youth room and taking notes . . . again. This kind of creativity shows how much Jarm takes training seriously.

Those who live in a more rural environment may have to use their imaginations a bit or at least be willing to travel to another town or city to accomplish what Jarm has done in his ministry. In addition to the football locker room and bank vault that Jarm mentions, we suggest going to local ministry locations, a hospital, the police station, a fire station, a nursing home, or even a cemetery to do some really cool training.

But don't forget to couple your creative training sessions with the one-on-one mentoring as Jarm does. You'll get a lot of miles out of the combination of these powerful elements.

Here is how we do ministry by teens in our youth ministry . . .

1. We start with preaching. In every sermon I preach to my youth, I encourage them to live what they're hearing by believing the gospel, following Jesus in obedience, loving each other, and reaching the lost.

2. We continue with community. We have our kids discuss what they heard, what they've read, and what God has done in their lives that relates to the teen worship service sermon that week. They're all in small groups, they open their Bibles, and they talk about how to apply these biblical truths in their lives and in their specific contexts.

3. This flows into ministry. We challenge all of our kids to go through a one-time one-month-long introduction class to spiritual gifts, which we call "You Got Skillz." In those classes we simply teach the storyline behind spiritual gifts (from Ephesians 4), the primary focus of spiritual gifts (the church), how to discern your spiritual giftedness (shape), and then how to identify which team the kids' particular gifts will fit with best.

4. Our training culminates with KTL ("Keruxon Ton Logon," which means "Preach the Word")—our twice-a-year leadership class for our kids. To be in this group, a teen must go through an application process. KTL in the fall teaches many different spiritual leadership characteristics through the study and discussion of leadership books. KTL in the spring teaches our youth guys how to preach and teach Scriptures, and our girls how to teach through the Scriptures. This class culminates with our top four guys preaching through a book of the Bible together in the month of April.

   A couple of other thoughts: We tell our youth all the time that our teen ministry wouldn't be nearly as effective, excellent, or cool without their using their giftedness on a weekly basis. About 20 percent of our teens end up being called into full-time ministry (all glory to Jesus), so I'm thankful this process is working for us!

—CHIP DEAN

OUR TAKE: *Did you catch that? Chip's teen leadership training begins and ends with preaching. First, he uses sermons to focus on leadership; and then, over the course of his training sessions, he prepares his kids to begin delivering their own sermons. So many youth workers assume they're the only ones who can (or should) do the preaching. It's refreshing to see a youth worker really model the "priesthood of all believers" mentality from 1 Peter 2:4–12.*

We have a leadership program, but "leadership" is almost a misnomer—the real purpose of this group is discipleship through leadership. We give kids a chance to lead the youth ministry, and we also pair them with individual mentors for reflection and prayer. Additionally, this serves the ministry well as the teens become well-known by another adult who isn't me (the youth pastor).

We train our teen leaders by having them read *Help! I'm a Student Leader!* (Doug Fields, Zondervan/Youth Specialties, 2005) during a retreat. Then we break into groups and have each teen teach a chapter. Also at this retreat, we have some bonding time; we plan a retreat for the entire youth group; and we work on administrative things, such as planning the next year's calendar, developing a phone tree, and so on.

Each teen is paired with a mentor. I pick the mentor for each teen based on both the teen's and the mentor's personality, experiences, background, hobbies, interests, and so on. God has really blessed this process, as I'm continually amazed by how the teens and mentors challenge each other and help each other grow to a new level.

In addition to spending time together at the monthly meetings, the mentors commit to one non-personal contact with their teen each month (such as email, phone call, card, and so on) and *at least* one personal contact a month (such as dinner, golf, bowling, hanging out after school, and seeing a movie). It's prudent to note that because of the one-on-one time, all of our mentors have undergone child protection training and been cleared by background checks.

We have monthly meetings comprised of all the leadership teens and all of the mentors. These meetings roughly break down into thirds:

1. We start off by eating a meal together. This builds community among the leadership teens and the adult mentors as well. It's a jovial time of bonding, laughing, and sharing.

2. Then we go into leadership time. We discuss upcoming events, plan retreats, discuss which kids have been absent lately and why, assign responsibilities for upcoming devotionals, and so on.

3. The final third of our time is spent in mentor pairs. This is where the magic happens. The teen and mentor spend time talking about life, sharing struggles, holding each other accountable, and praying together. Originally we budgeted less than 20 minutes for this prayer time, but it quickly grew to where the teens and mentors were spending an *hour* and 20 minutes sharing and praying for each other.

—TOM BUTLER

OUR TAKE: Tom is really building momentum with adult-influenced teen leaders. It seems as though he pairs godly adult leaders with kids at every turn. It's really exciting to see how he calls his adult leaders to some form of connection with their teenagers outside of regular youth ministry events (like golf, bowling, and so on).

Tom is also taking great care in how he blends adults with kids. He mentions a background check, and we highly recommend that you perform one on every adult leader in your ministry, too. In fact, some denominations have made this a requirement for ministry—even for volunteers. Check into this to make sure you're compliant; then pair loving adults with teens who need them.

One of the most effective tools I use is giving my teen leaders the opportunity to preach throughout the year. I walk with them through the process, help them put it together, and then allow them to lead their fellow youth from the pulpit.

This has provided such encouragement for both the adult leaders and the youth. Even here in Australia—where we like to bag each other out pretty much all the time—this is a time when the teen leaders are cheered on and encouraged. They spend time in the Bible, and it stretches them in their faith and reliance upon God. We've had a number of teen leaders from our church go into Bible college to enter full-time ministry.

—MARK REILLY

OUR TAKE: Wow! Here's another youth worker who uses preaching as both a motivation and evidence of teenage leadership. Perhaps this is something all of us should take a hard look at as we develop and refine our teen leadership ministries.

I came to this position in January 2008. For the first several months, I observed the teens and what they were all about—just as I'm sure they were observing me. After some prayer God gave me the names of four teens who could be used in a leadership capacity. I didn't do any formal training, but I did give them a list of what it takes to be a teen leader. Before they came aboard, they had to pray about it and make sure they could do what was on the list I'd given to them:

Expectations of a Teenage Leader
1. Be a disciple and conduct yourself in a way that honors God. (Be the example.)
2. Maintain a personal quiet time, participate in worship, and encourage other kids to do the same.
3. Witness to peers, leading them to faith in Jesus Christ and regular church attendance.
4. Greet and interact with new teen visitors when they come to church.
5. Help plan, promote, and participate in all functions we do as a youth group and other functions as needed.
6. Encourage other kids to get involved not only in all Bible studies, but also in all youth events.
7. Be personally involved in the Bible studies, encouraging peers to be personally involved as well.
8. Attend planning meetings for upcoming events as needed.
9. Be willing to lead a Bible study if called upon.
10. Be a humble follower.

But what I really want to tell you is that these four kids had their own ideas about what they wanted to do with their lives. But after putting them in some leadership positions, three of the four have asked God what God wants them to do and are now listening to what God has in store for them.

One went from wanting to be an art major to wanting to study biblical counseling; another went from being an English major to becoming a missionary; and a third went from not knowing what he wanted to do to wanting to become a youth pastor. I truly believe these results are from putting the kids in leadership roles and seeing how it all works. They realized what it takes to truly follow Jesus and what he wants.

—GEORGE GRACIE

OUR TAKE: George's list of expectations is a good one, though it could use a little emphasis on teen leadership outside the youth group. The main thing is that he held his kids to a godly standard, and that played a big part in these teens' turning their lives over more fully to God's leading and direction.

Our purpose is to help any willing person become his or her best for Jesus Christ. We have a PIT (Pastor in Training) program, a MIT (Missionary in Training) program, and a LIT (Leader in Training) program.

When a high schooler feels called into the possibility of leadership ministry, she enters the LIT program, where she'll experience a wide variety of ministries suited to her talents and the church's needs. The LIT kids discover the inner workings of the local church and the importance of every ministry.

After high school they can enter the MIT or PIT programs if they feel called to do so.

MIT participants work throughout the church learning to relate to people, organize, evangelize, teach, and preach. They gain experience by helping with the biannual mission conference and interacting with veteran missionaries and our missionary board.

The PIT program is for those who want to prepare themselves for pastoral ministry. They teach, preach, assist in worship services, and exercise leadership in various ministries while attending college or seminary.

PIT participants are exposed to the inner workings of church life and the multifaceted duties of a pastor. Their training enables them to see if they're indeed fit and ready for pastoral ministry. PIT trainees may attend staff meetings, pastors' meetings, and board meetings and are exposed to a host of other learning opportunities.

—BRIAN MCDANIEL

OUR TAKE: Brian's model is a superb one; it offers teens three very different opportunities to serve God in ministry. It's refreshing to see a youth worker make an intentional effort to produce missionaries and pastors from within the confines of a youth group. It's not easy, as I'm sure Brian would attest, but we can never lose sight of the fact that the next generation of pastors and missionaries is sitting in our small groups right now.

I started our teen leadership program—nicknamed "Life 360"—as a weekly time to connect with the kids I saw as leaders, and looking at 360 degrees of life—what we take in and what we put out. I prayerfully handpicked five diverse kids—two from a Catholic school, two from other local high schools, and one who's homeschooled. I wanted to work with developing leaders for each setting.

From that point on, the group has adapted—some have moved beyond this program and others have joined. I've always tried to keep around five kids in the leadership group. The neat thing is that they're so committed to the program that *they* decided we should meet at 7:00 a.m. once a week before school because it was difficult to work around everyone's schedules.
This is our monthly routine:

Week One—connect over breakfast or coffee to find out how everyone's doing.

Week Two—it's all about God's Word (the Bible), either as a group study or some individual time.

Week Three—our week to serve others, where we write letters of encouragement, serve breakfast to kids on their way to school, shovel snow (ugh!), and so on.

Week Four—a training week on various topics, such as how to talk to your friends about God, and so on.

Week Five is called "surprise." Since there aren't many "week fives" throughout the year, we save those for something really special, crazy, and fun!

—JEREL PETERS

OUR TAKE: Jerel's well-rounded approach is something we can all benefit from, although we believe his most important offering to all of us is the mind-set of looking at 360 degrees of our young people's lives. Teenagers—even teen leaders—need someone in their lives who will take a hard look at who they are, what they're doing, and where they're headed.

It's also good to see that Jerel has built some intentional service times into his teen leaders' agendas. At some point teen leaders have to make an impact on others, or else they aren't really leaders. Service projects are a great way to offer this experience.

We've developed SOS (Spirit of Service), a teen leadership group. Our kids and their parents sign a contract to commit the teens to a full year of service. Afterward they attend training on Christian leadership to understand the specifics of the jobs we have them do. We incorporate teaching on the different passions and spiritual gifts necessary for each job. After completing the training, the kids receive photo ID badges to wear every week.

The jobs range from greeting and playing with our early childhood Sunday school students to doughnut and drink duty during fellowship with their peers, and game prep, assistance, and cleanup for elementary students. These jobs take place every Sunday when children arrive at church and while our teachers prepare the morning lesson. That means the teens in SOS give up their fellowship time every Sunday to serve others.

Our teachers who are assisted by SOS kids are overwhelmingly thankful for the help provided. The younger children have teens to look up to, bridging the generation gap and allowing them to see that even kids can serve with joyful hearts.

We have an occasional ice-cream sundae party and other special events for our kids in SOS, showing our appreciation for them and encouraging them along the way. The younger kids really look forward to becoming leaders in SOS.

—NICOLE DARR

OUR TAKE: Did you notice how Nicole identified a gap in her teen leadership? She noted that her leaders were sacrificially forfeiting their fellowship time, so she built that component into her teen leadership ministry. You really can use something as simple as an ice-cream party to thank your teen leaders. The time they get to spend with you—their youth worker—is probably more important to them than the sweets.

Our teen leadership program is called the "Student Influence Team." We use teen leaders as our small group Bible study leaders. We give them kid-friendly curricula, and they prepare the lesson each week, often editing the questions to better fit our group or sometimes taking the lesson in a better direction than where the original curriculum pointed. The teens lead the discussion (adult participants are present but let the teens lead).

After the small-group time is over, we do leadership training with the teen leaders for 15 minutes. We discuss what went well, what they can improve upon, with whom to follow up, and general leadership training issues. We train them before the semester starts by teaching them how our small group format works, how to lead a good small group, and how leaders live.

In addition to the small group leaders mentioned above, we have a handful of kids who help plan, set up, and tear down events, as well as reach out to people we haven't seen for a few weeks. We talk to these teens about how they help us create our culture at teenage ministry gatherings and events.

—BRIAN SWANSON

OUR TAKE: Again, we're seeing youth pastors emphasizing teenagers teaching their peers in the ministry, and that's really cool. Hey, how else will they be prepared to do it on college campuses? We also really like how Brian's adults instantly provide feedback to their teen leaders. As we said in earlier chapters, this is crucial for the further development of our teenagers. Yeah, it requires a little extra time each week, but that deposit is making a huge investment in teenage leaders.

I found myself in a situation where there were no willing, committed adults to serve as youth leaders. However, I had two mature teens (Lisa and Christina) who were ready to start serving. I felt led by God to make them the teen leadership team (along with myself) to plan events for the youth.

I first took them with my family to a youth pastors' conference held by my denomination. It gave us time to spend together but also served as a reward for them. (That trip had the best speakers and musicians!) During one meal, I shared with them my vision for our youth and then "commissioned" them as teen leaders (which simply means I prayed for them).

From that point on, I met with them about once a month—both to equip them for youth ministry and to plan our events. The equipping involved using articles found from various youth resources, including www.thesource4ym.com. I even assigned them certain events where they would be in charge of all the details and I would only serve in an advisory role.

Delegating events turned out to be a huge success! Lisa planned a fundraiser for our youth camp. She planned the meal for after church and went all out in decorating the fellowship hall with a beach theme (using only items that she already owned). Our church of 100 attendees raised over $600! And it gave Lisa a chance to use her gift of administration.

Christina also did a great job. She organized a fellowship activity consisting of the youth going out of town to eat at a nice restaurant. The event went a long way in forming close relationships among our members. Christina also became my backup teacher for Sunday school, utilizing her gift of teaching. I'm so glad God led me to use teens as a part of my ministry.

—DIZZY FELKEL

OUR TAKE: *It's fantastic to see how Dizzy paid attention and keyed in on the girls' gifts and strengths and allowed them to serve in areas where they'd be the biggest blessing to their peers. Also, Dizzy's story strongly illustrates how teen leaders can grow in their capacity of responsibility. The girls moved from decorating and hosting parties all the way up to teaching. That sort of growth happens best when, as Dizzy did, we spend time with our teenage leaders.*

DOING IT

All of these ministries have one thing in common: They didn't stop at just *noticing* the need for teen leadership—they *acted* on it.

My guess is that you've been energized by reading this chapter and learning what real ministries are doing across the world. These ministries all started somewhere. They had a *desire* to see ministry by teens—and they *acted* on it.

Now it's up to you. *Noticing* a need is important. Being *excited* is even better. But it doesn't stop there. It's actually a matter of *doing it*. There's more than enough in this book to help you get started with what God wants to accomplish in your ministries.

What are you waiting for?

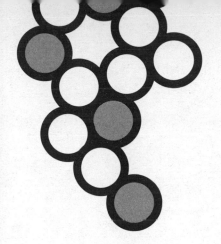

APPENDIX

LEADERSHIP TRAINING RETREAT SCHEDULE

THE NATURE OF LEADERS

This blueprint is designed to be used in a weekend retreat structure. You don't have to use it that way, but the verbiage follows that intent.

We've created a collection of three different sessions to help you teach your kids about the nature of leaders. In the first session, you'll talk about leaders being people of faith. In the second session, you'll lead a discussion about the fact that leaders should have ambition to change the world. And in the third and final session, you'll talk about sacrifice.

If you choose to use these sessions in a weekend format, here's a possible schedule you could follow to guide you through the weekend:

FRIDAY

6:00 p.m.
Arrive at camp
Unpack
Eat dinner
7:30 p.m.
Session One
9:00 p.m.
Snacks and hang time
11:00 p.m.
Lights out

SATURDAY

8:00 a.m.
Breakfast
9:00 a.m.
Session Two
10:30 a.m.
Activity One (team builder)
12:00 p.m.
Lunch
1:30 p.m.
Activity Two (team builder or use of a camp amenity)
3:00 p.m.
Free time
5:30 p.m.
Dinner
7:00 p.m.
Special Outing (dinner, bowling, concert, laser tag)*
11:00 p.m.
Lights out

SUNDAY

8:00 a.m.
Breakfast
9:00 a.m.
Session Three
10:30 a.m.
Pack and load up
11:30 a.m.
Head for home

Don't skimp on the special outing on Saturday night. You don't have to spend a ton of money—but engineer something special. You can bring a video projector and show a movie on the lawn, or you can take the leaders out for a show and ice cream. This will be a fantastic time of fellowship. Make the most of it.

In the session outlines that follow, you're given a discussion starter for launching into your group time. The discussion starters include an activity, a music video, and a video clip from a movie. The sessions also include biblical passages and small group questions based on the passage and topic. Finally, each session concludes with a takeaway that wraps up the session in a neat package.

SESSION ONE:
LEADERS MUST BE FILLED WITH FAITH

MAIN POINT: Teens must exemplify a high level of faith in their personal lives if they're going to be spiritual leaders.

ACTIVITY DISCUSSION STARTER: Taking a step of faith. Relax; this isn't the same old "fall off a chair backward and let the group catch you in their arms" gimmick. This activity does teach your teen leaders about faith, but it employs a different tactic and uses everyone in the group.

You'll need the following items for every five kids:
15 regular balloons (just normal party balloons)
One eight-foot-long table

Begin by handing out three balloons to each teen leader as you begin your session. Instruct them to blow up the balloons to the same size and then tie them off. When all of the balloons are inflated and tied, ask the teen leaders to come to the front of the room with their balloons.

Before the session begins, you'll need to have the eight-foot table positioned at the front of the room and turned upside down so the legs are sticking up (or folded inside the table). Have the teens place their balloons under the surface of the table (between it and the floor) and then return to their seats. At this point you should have at least 15 balloons under the table, and you'll want to make sure the balloons are evenly distributed.

Ask your kids if they believe the table will hold them.

After they answer, bring up one of your teen leaders and help her stand on top of the table (which is actually the bottom because it's upside down). If the balloons are properly inflated and tied off—and if you've evenly spread them out under the table—the teen will be able to stand on the table without any problems at all.

Without letting the first person step off the table, ask the other leaders if they think the table can hold another person. Then allow a second kid to join the first one on top of the table.

Continue this process with as many kids as possible until you can't fit any more onto the table. One or two balloons may pop, but you should be able to get everyone on the table. Most of the kids will assume that when they get onto the table, the balloons will pop. They'll be very surprised.

TRANSITION STATEMENT

Sometimes we doubt God and God's power. If our faith isn't very strong, we begin to think, "God can't handle the situation I'm facing," or, "I don't think God can accomplish his purpose through me because it's so big and I'm so small." In every part of life, including our moments of doubt, it's important to remember that we must have faith.

It's even more important for us as leaders. God wants to use us to accomplish great things for God's kingdom. I promise you one thing—to be a leader, you must have faith. So let's spend the next few moments talking about faith.

DISCUSSION QUESTIONS

1. AROUND THE CIRCLE: As we kick off our weekend, let's all take a second to share our names and our favorite things to do for fun.

2. ASK A FEW: What did you think was going to happen when the first person got on top of the table?

3. ASK A FEW: How many kids did you think the balloon-supported table could hold?

4. ASK A FEW: When it came time for you to step onto the table, how much faith did it require?

5. ASK A FEW: Was this activity like life? How?

6. ASK A FEW: Is it difficult to do things when they don't make sense?

7. ASK A FEW: Do God's ways always make sense to us?

Read the following passage:

Now faith is being sure of what we hope for and certain of what we do not see. This is what the ancients were commended for.

CONTINUED ON NEXT PAGE

By faith we understand that the universe was formed at God's command, so that what is seen was not made out of what was visible.

By faith Abel brought God a better offering than Cain did. By faith he was commended as righteous, when God spoke well of his offerings. And by faith Abel still speaks, even though he is dead.

By faith Enoch was taken from this life, so that he did not experience death: "He could not be found, because God had taken him away." For before he was taken, he was commended as one who pleased God. And without faith it is impossible to please God, because anyone who comes to him must believe that he exists and that he rewards those who earnestly seek him.

By faith Noah, when warned about things not yet seen, in holy fear built an ark to save his family. By his faith he condemned the world and became heir of the righteousness that is in keeping with faith.

By faith Abraham, when called to go to a place he would later receive as his inheritance, obeyed and went, even though he did not know where he was going. By faith he made his home in the promised land like a stranger in a foreign country; he lived in tents, as did Isaac and Jacob, who were heirs with him of the same promise. For he was looking forward to the city with foundations, whose architect and builder is God. And by faith even Sarah, who was past childbearing age, was enabled to bear children because she considered him faithful who had made the promise. And so from this one man, and he as good as dead, came descendants as numerous as the stars in the sky and as countless as the sand on the seashore.

All these people were still living by faith when they died. They did not receive the things promised; they only saw them and welcomed them from a distance, admitting that they were foreigners and strangers on earth. People who say such things show that they are looking for a country of their own. If they had been thinking of the country they had left, they would have had opportunity to return. Instead, they were longing for a better country—a heavenly one. Therefore God is not ashamed to be called their God, for he has prepared a city for them.

By faith Abraham, when God tested him, offered Isaac as a sacrifice. He who had embraced the promises was about to sacrifice his one and only son, even though God had said to him, "It is through Isaac that your offspring will be reckoned." Abraham reasoned that God could even raise the dead, and so in a manner of speaking he did receive Isaac back from death.

By faith Isaac blessed Jacob and Esau in regard to their future.

By faith Jacob, when he was dying, blessed each of Joseph's sons, and worshiped as he leaned on the top of his staff.

By faith Joseph, when his end was near, spoke about the exodus of the Israelites from Egypt and gave instructions concerning the burial of his bones.

By faith Moses' parents hid him for three months after he was born, because they saw he was no ordinary child, and they were not afraid of the king's edict.

By faith Moses, when he had grown up, refused to be known as the son of Pharaoh's daughter. He chose to be mistreated along with the people of God rather than to enjoy the fleeting pleasures of sin. He regarded disgrace for the sake of Christ as of greater value than the treasures of Egypt, because he was looking ahead to his reward. By faith he left Egypt, not fearing the king's anger; he persevered because he saw him who is invisible. By faith he kept the Passover and the application of blood, so that the destroyer of the firstborn would not touch the firstborn of Israel.

By faith the people passed through the Red Sea as on dry land; but when the Egyptians tried to do so, they were drowned.

By faith the walls of Jericho fell, after the army had marched around them for seven days.

By faith the prostitute Rahab, because she welcomed the spies, was not killed with those who were disobedient.

And what more shall I say? I do not have time to tell about Gideon, Barak, Samson and Jephthah, about David and Samuel and the prophets, who through faith conquered kingdoms, administered justice, and gained what was promised; who shut the mouths of lions, quenched the fury of the flames, and escaped the edge of the sword; whose weakness was turned to strength; and who became powerful in battle and routed foreign armies. Women received back their dead, raised to life again. There were others who were tortured, refusing to be released so that they might gain an even better resurrection. Some faced jeers and flogging, and even chains and imprisonment. They were put to death by stoning; they were sawed in two; they were killed by the sword. They went about in sheepskins and goatskins, destitute, persecuted and mistreated—the world was not worthy of them. They wandered in deserts and mountains, and in caves and holes in the ground.

These were all commended for their faith, yet none of them received what had been promised. God had planned something better for us so that only together with us would they be made perfect. (Hebrews 11:1–40)

8. **ASK SOMEONE: How does this passage describe and define faith?**

9. **ASK A FEW: Since all of us are ministry leaders, we should be familiar with most of the stories referenced in Hebrews 11, also**

known as the "Hall of Faith." Which is your favorite and why? *(If you have time, you may want to break into smaller groups and have each team read the unfamiliar stories and brief each other on them.)*

10. ASK A FEW: Which of the leaders from this list had to have the most faith? Why?

11. ASK A FEW: Which of the leaders from this chapter can you identify with the most? The least?

12. ASK A FEW: Reread verse 13. How does that make you feel?

13. ASK A FEW: Take a moment and describe the faith of any one of these individuals from Hebrews 11 and why that person's life was important to others.

14. ASK A FEW: These people were leaders in one way or another. They also had faith. Since you're going to be a leader in our ministry, what must you do to have faith similar to theirs?

15. AROUND THE CIRCLE: What usually keeps you from having faith in God and God's Word to you?

16. AROUND THE CIRCLE: What will you do immediately to begin to have more faith and trust God more?

TAKEAWAY

The leaders in the Bible changed the world as much as anyone else in the history of humanity. They weren't always the strongest, the smartest, the wisest, the richest, or the best. But the people God used had one thing in common: Strong faith.

Since we're leaders, then like these biblical heroes we must also exemplify faith. That's not to say we do stupid stuff and have false hope—like jumping off a building and thinking we can fly. But having faith does mean that when God speaks, we obey—no matter how challenging or weird God's call may sound.

I say this because, as leaders, we're going to face plenty of times when we'll need faith. If we want God to use us—and we all do—then we have to be prepared to follow God in all things. And that requires faith!

A moment ago I asked you what needed to change about your life so you could have more faith. I also asked you what you should change immediately to begin living a life of stronger faith. We're going to close out our session tonight in prayer with one another, lifting up those needs together.

(Don't be in any hurry here. Just divide the group into smaller teams and have them pray for their needs and for one another. You might even have them pray for the weekend. Just spend some time in prayer, asking God to help you grow in faith.)

[This session is based on an idea that Andy Matzke submitted to www.thesource4ym.com.]

SESSION TWO:
LEADERS CHANGE THE WORLD

MAIN POINT: God has called us to be leaders, so we must do our part to help God change the world!

MUSIC VIDEO DISCUSSION STARTER: "If Everyone Cared" by Nickelback (You can easily download the music video from iTunes.)

Even though the album *All the Right Reasons* dropped in October of 2005, several of its songs are still getting lots of radio playtime today. As a matter of fact, the album peaked at number one and spent at least 145 weeks in the top 100! *Yeah, it's a popular album.*

Hailing from Canada, the group made a name for themselves in 2001 when the single "How You Remind Me" was released. Today, with more than 14 million albums sold and trophies collected from the MTV Video Music Awards, the World Music Awards, the Billboard Music Awards, and the Juno Awards, Nickelback is still reaping the rewards of *All the Right Reasons*. In addition to "If Everyone Cared," the love ballad "Far Away" and the celebrity-laden but raunchy-messaged music video "Rockstar" are also popular tunes from this disc.

Nickelback is famous and talented but not always appropriate. From "Fight for All the Wrong Reasons" to "Animals" to "Side of a Bullet," the band issues its fair share of dangerous messages. Their lyrics are often laced with sex, jealousy, sex, violence, and sex. Though many youth workers have wanted to turn Nickelback off for the past five years, remember—lots of kids have chosen to turn them up.

It's possible to teach teen leaders about God and God's calling using Nickelback's music video without actually endorsing their music to your teenagers. (The practice of using secular material for sacred purposes goes all the way back to the apostle Paul. See Acts 17.)

Note to Leader: This music discussion uses two large passages of Scripture. Additionally, there are two portions of context notes for you to share with your group that will help the story make more sense. So you should allow about 45 minutes for the small group discussion time (which comes after your introduction, the music video, and your transition statement).

INTRODUCING THE MUSIC VIDEO: While passing out a copy of the song's lyrics (which you can access from the Internet), say, **Here's a copy of the lyrics from one of Nickelback's songs entitled "If Everyone Cared." If you need to follow along on your sheet, that's fine; but make sure you pay attention to the actual video so we can talk about the stories later.**

TRANSITION STATEMENT

This music video showed the stories of several leaders who did their part to change the world. Maybe you didn't know it, but that's our job as Christian leaders—changing the world. Let's take a look at a story from the Bible about a young girl who helped change the world in a very important way.

SMALL GROUP TIME

Say, **Let's go ahead and split up into our discussion groups. Afterward, we'll come back together for a final word.**

(See www.thesource4ym.com/howdoi/smallgroups.asp for a quick training article on how to maximize your small groups using our small-group format—a great resource to equip your small group leaders.)

DISCUSSION QUESTIONS

1. **AROUND THE CIRCLE: As we get started, I'd like everybody to share their favorite singer or music group.**

2. **ASK A FEW: What does the singer mean when he says, "If everyone cared and nobody cried, If everyone loved and nobody lied, If everyone shared and swallowed their pride, Then we'd see the day when nobody died"?**

3. **ASK A FEW: Can anyone list the names of the people in the video who helped "save the world"? (Leaders—below is a list of**

the people whom the video highlights, along with their life's major accomplishments.)

Bob Geldof—he was a music journalist who started a band. After hearing about starvation in Africa, he hosted multiple concerts around the world simultaneously, raising $150 million in one day. Those concerts continue to this day, fighting world hunger.

Betty Williams—she was a mom and a secretary who saw three children die in the terrible violence in Northern Ireland. Just a couple of days later, she organized a peace walk for 10,000 people, but protestors violently broke it up. One week after that, she returned with 35,000 marchers! For her efforts, she won the Nobel Peace Prize in 1976.

Peter Benenson—he was a British lawyer who helped college students in Portugal realize their freedom. His mission was so greatly needed that it grew into a worldwide effort called Amnesty International. Still in place today, Amnesty International helps millions and millions fight for human rights.

Nelson Mandela—he watched oppression and murder run rampant in South Africa for years. When he tried to intervene, he was arrested, beaten, and imprisoned for 27 years. When he was finally released in 1990, he led his country through its first free voting process in history. South Africa is a different country today because of his lifelong work.

4. **ASK A FEW: What are some of the qualities these people have in common?**

5. **ASK A FEW: Do you know anybody else in history who has changed the world or maybe even helped save it?**

6. **ASK A FEW: Okay. Great list! Now tell me—how would the world be different today if those people hadn't stepped up?**

7. **ASK A FEW: As the music video ended, this quote from Margaret Mead came on the screen: "Never doubt that a small group of committed people can change the world. Indeed, it is the only thing that ever has." Do you think this is true? Why or why not?**

8. ASK A FEW: Do you think God is involved in changing the world? If so, how?

Say, I want us to read part of a story from the Bible about a person who changed the world. But before we do, let me give you some background info.

King Xerxes liked to party—a lot. He'd throw parties that lasted 180 days, and then he'd throw parties that lasted a week—just to end the big party. He had a wife named Queen Vashti. She liked to party, too. Often-times while Xerxes was throwing a party for the guys, Vashti was throwing one for the women.

One day, Xerxes called for Vashti to join him at his party, but she snubbed him; she didn't show up. This really made Xerxes mad, and he kicked her out of the kingdom.

Then he had his officials search for another queen to take her place. They found Esther, a Jewish girl—one of God's chosen people—and Xerxes chose her to be the next queen. One of the interesting things about Esther was that she had an uncle named Mordecai, who was also Jewish, who'd raised her and was helping take care of her while she was queen. And he told Esther never to tell anyone that she was a Jew, including King Xerxes. (At this time in history, the Jews were actually being held as captives, and they were hated by many people. So it was dangerous to be a Jew during Esther's day.)

Everything was going pretty well until a bad guy, Haman, entered the scene. He was the second in command and on a HUGE ego trip. Wherever he went, people would bow down to him. Everybody except Mordecai, that is. This really angered Haman. It made him so mad that he wanted to kill Mordecai. But when Haman found out that Mordecai was a Jew, he decided to kill Mordecai and every other Jew in the land!

Haman knew he couldn't do this without King Xerxes' permission, so he pulled a fast one and got King Xerxes to send a decree throughout the land that gave Haman's henchmen permission to kill all of the Jews (including Mordecai and Queen Esther).

Mordecai heard the news concerning the destruction of his people. He ripped off his clothes, put on sackcloth, and sat at the city gate mourning his people's fate. That's where our story picks up in the Bible.

Read the following passage:

Then Esther summoned Hathak, one of the king's eunuchs assigned to attend her, and ordered him to find out what was troubling Mordecai and why.

So Hathak went out to Mordecai in the open square of the city in front of the king's gate. Mordecai told him everything that had happened to him, including the exact amount of money Haman had promised to pay into the royal treasury for the destruction of the Jews. He also gave him a copy of the text of the edict for their annihilation, which had been published in Susa, to show to Esther and explain it to her, and he told him to instruct her to go into the king's presence to beg for mercy and plead with him for her people.

Hathak went back and reported to Esther what Mordecai had said. Then she instructed him to say to Mordecai, "All the king's officials and the people of the royal provinces know that for any man or woman who approaches the king in the inner court without being summoned the king has but one law: that they be put to death unless the king extends the gold scepter to them and spares their lives. But thirty days have passed since I was called to go to the king."

When Esther's words were reported to Mordecai, he sent back this answer: "Do not think that because you are in the king's house you alone of all the Jews will escape. For if you remain silent at this time, relief and deliverance for the Jews will arise from another place, but you and your father's family will perish. And who knows but that you have come to royal position for such a time as this?"

Then Esther sent this reply to Mordecai: "Go, gather together all the Jews who are in Susa, and fast for me. Do not eat or drink for three days, night or day. I and my attendants will fast as you do. When this is done, I will go to the king, even though it is against the law. And if I perish, I perish."

So Mordecai went away and carried out all of Esther's instructions. (Esther 4:5–17)

9. **ASK SOMEONE: Do you think Esther and Mordecai's plans qualify as changing the world? Why or why not?**

10. **ASK SOMEONE: What kept Esther from wanting to help at first? In other words, what was she afraid of?** *(Hint: See verse 11. She could die just for entering the king's presence without his permission.)*

11. **ASK A FEW: What do you think are some of the necessary characteristics of people who change the world?**

12. **ASK A FEW: Do you think you could've done what Esther planned to do? Why or why not?**

Next say, **Let's take a few minutes to see how the story ended. But again, let me fill in some of the blanks between chapters 4 and 7.**

As Mordecai and Esther tried to save their people from destruction, Esther pulled out all the stops, got all dressed up, and humbly approached the king's throne with a secret weapon—an invitation to a rockin' party! Haman was also invited. Well, there was no way Xerxes was turning down a party, so both he and Haman went.

At the party King Xerxes asked Esther what she wanted of him. She really poured it on and said, "I just want you to have such a good time at my party that you'll come back for another party tomorrow." Well, because Xerxes was a party addict, he didn't refuse her request. The party ended, and everybody went home.

But Xerxes couldn't sleep that night, so he had a servant bring him a copy of the official records of the kingdom so he could read to make himself sleepy. While reading it, he found a story of how Mordecai had actually saved his life by blowing the whistle on an assassination plot! Xerxes asked the servant what was done to show Mordecai the king's gratitude. The servant reported that nothing was ever done.

So Xerxes called in Haman (in the middle of the night) and asked him what should be done for a person whom the king wants to honor. Thinking the king was talking about him, Haman rolled out a list of cool things.

Then Xerxes said, "Great! You go do all of these things you just said—for MORDECAI!"

Haman did so because the king had commanded him, but he was so angry he could hardly stand it. Well, things were about to get even worse for him because it was time for the second party. Let's see what happened.

Read the following passage:

So the king and Haman went to Queen Esther's banquet, and as they were drinking wine on the second day, the king again asked, "Queen Esther, what is your petition? It will be given you. What is your request? Even up to half the kingdom, it will be granted."

Then Queen Esther answered, "If I have found favor with you, Your Majesty, and if it pleases you, grant me my life—this is my petition. And spare my people—this is my request. For I and my people have been sold to be destroyed, killed and annihilated. If we had merely been sold as male and female slaves, I would have kept quiet, because no such distress would justify disturbing the king."

King Xerxes asked Queen Esther, "Who is he? Where is he—the man who has dared to do such a thing?"

Esther said, "An adversary and enemy! This vile Haman!"

Then Haman was terrified before the king and queen. The king got up in a rage, left his wine and went out into the palace garden. But Haman, realizing that the king had already decided his fate, stayed behind to beg Queen Esther for his life.

Just as the king returned from the palace garden to the banquet hall, Haman was falling on the couch where Esther was reclining.

The king exclaimed, "Will he even molest the queen while she is with me in the house?"

As soon as the word left the king's mouth, they covered Haman's face. Then Harbona, one of the eunuchs attending the king, said, "A pole reaching to a height of fifty cubits stands by Haman's house. He had it set up for Mordecai, who spoke up to help the king."

The king said, "Impale him on it!" So they impaled Haman on the pole he had set up for Mordecai. Then the king's fury subsided. (Esther 7:1–10)

13. **ASK SOMEONE: So were Mordecai and Esther successful? (Yes. In the end the bad guy got it; and in the next few chapters, we're told that the king reversed his orders to have all the Jews killed because it was all Haman's idea in the first place.)**

14. **ASK A FEW: Did you know that the word *God* isn't found even ONE time in the entire book of Esther? Even though that's the case, do you think God played a role in this story? Why or why not?**

15. **ASK A FEW: As leaders, when you look around today, do you see things about the world that need to be changed? If so, what are they?**

16. **ASK A FEW: What will you do about it starting NOW?**

TAKEAWAY

So we just watched a fairly compelling video about people who looked into the faces of other hurting people and were stirred enough to do something to change the situation. We say those people changed the world. Other people changed our world, too. Martin Luther King Jr. fought for the rights of African Americans during the 1950s and 1960s. The Allied powers of America, Britain, France, and Russia helped free Europe from Hitler's stranglehold in the 1940s. Mother Teresa cared for the impoverished people in the ghettos of Calcutta. The list goes on and on.

Then we looked at a great story from the Bible about a girl named Esther who changed the world. She saved her people, the Jews, from annihilation. With help from her Uncle Mordecai—and God—she did her part to make sure millions and millions of people would be alive today.

All of these people lived heroes' lives. But one stands head and shoulders above the rest: Jesus. The Bible tells us that Jesus saw the shame, pain, and suffering of all people brought on by their sin. He decided something must be done to change the world—to save the world! So he came to us and taught us about God, his Father. He taught us about love and grace and mercy. He healed many people from diseases and sicknesses. A few times, Jesus even raised people from the dead. His love for all of us compelled him to give his life on a cross to take away our sins so not only could we have a relationship with God now, but also in heaven. Though Jesus died, three days later God raised him to life again.

And on top of all that Jesus has done for us, he invites us—ministry leaders—to join him in changing the world and, when necessary, saving the world.

In our discussion we talked about ways in which you think the world needs to be changed. If you have ANY ambition to serve people and change the world, *you'll need God's help*. That's the faith element we talked about in our last session.

God's business is saving the world. And God wants to do it through you as a leader. Are you ready?

Close in prayer.

[This discussion is based on an idea submitted by Tyler to www.thesource4ym.com.]

SESSION THREE:
LEADERS MUST BE SACRIFICIAL

MAIN POINT: Leaders make sacrifices for those who follow them.

MOVIE CLIP DISCUSSION STARTER: "You're willing to exchange your life for theirs?" *Hart's War*, starring Bruce Willis and Colin Farrell, is a great movie about honor, bravery, and sacrifice. Set in a German POW camp during World War II, this movie helps us understand what sacrifice means.

INTRODUCING THE CLIP: I want to show you a clip from the movie *Hart's War*. Colin Farrell plays Lt. Thomas W. Hart, a young World War II officer with a cushy job. While on a routine delivery one day, he's ambushed, taken prisoner, tortured, and sent to a POW camp. There he meets Col. William A. McNamara (played by Bruce Willis), a fourth-generation soldier whose toughness is rivaled only by his cleverness. Col. McNamara is also the leader for all of the American prisoners at the POW camp.

The Americans continue to fight the war from behind the fences and plan an escape to destroy a nearby munitions plant. Every perceived act of rebellion by the prisoners is met with extreme retaliation. The Nazis execute random prisoners for discipline, discouraging any attempts to escape. A murder in camp, a mock court-martial, and racial tension provide them with the chance to set a plan in motion. Everyone, especially McNamara, understands and is willing to accept the consequences for an escape attempt.

The stage has been set, the players are in place, and the trial is nearing its end. McNamara and 34 men are escaping while Hart delivers his closing arguments. Even though he's innocent, Hart confesses to the murder, willing to sacrifice himself. This leads to the Nazis' discovery of the escape attempt.

Let's watch the dramatic ending of *Hart's War*.

Scene Script:
Begin clip at one hour, 51 minutes, and 59 seconds.

Visser:	I want every man . . . who participated in the court-martial . . . removed from the line. Line them up. Line them up. Now!
Hart:	These men knew nothing, Colonel.
Visser:	Line them up! You will be the first.
Hart:	These men knew nothing.
Visser:	You will be the first!
Hart:	Colonel, they knew nothing!
Visser:	So your men are saboteurs as well?
McNamara:	No, Colonel, they're just soldiers. They were following my orders. I assume complete responsibility.
Visser:	That's very noble of you. Seems you've won our duel after all, Colonel.
McNamara:	No. We both lose, don't we?
Visser:	Yeah. And now you wish to trade your life for theirs?
McNamara:	Yes, I do.
Visser:	Very well.

End clip at one hour, 56 minutes, and 38 seconds. *(Please note: There's a graphic scene of violence right after this clip, so be prepared to stop it at the appropriate time.)*

TRANSITION STATEMENT

Our culture loves heroic sacrifice. We want to celebrate those who are willing to give themselves for their country, their family, their friends, and yes, even for God. I think you'll find that your peers in our ministry also love stories of sacrifice. So we must be willing to be leaders who sacrifice for their sake and God's. The good news is that our sacrifice is always used by God to accomplish God's purposes.

DISCUSSION QUESTIONS

1. AROUND THE CIRCLE: Let's share our highs and lows real quick. Just tell everyone the high and low points of your weekend so far.

2. ASK A FEW: What did you feel when you saw Col. McNamara standing at the gate?

3. ASK A FEW: Why do you think Col. McNamara came back to the camp once he was out?

4. ASK A FEW: How do you think Col. McNamara's men felt when they saw him come back?

5. ASK SOMEONE: What was the result of McNamara's sacrifice? (Hart and the other solders got to live.)

Read the following passage:

This is how we know what love is: Jesus Christ laid down his life for us. And we ought to lay down our lives for one another. If any one of you has material possessions and sees a brother or sister in need but has no pity on them, how can the love of God be in you? Dear children, let us not love with words or tongue but with actions and in truth. (1 John 3:16–18)

6. ASK SOMEONE: According to this passage, how can we know what love is?

7. ASK A FEW: What does it mean that Jesus laid down his life?

8. ASK A FEW: How is what Col. McNamara did the same thing? How is it different?

9. ASK A FEW: We're told in this passage not just to love one another with words or tongue, but with actions and in truth. What does that mean?

10. ASK SOMEONE: What was the result of Jesus' sacrifice? (We were given eternal life.)

11. ASK A FEW: What effect should Jesus' sacrifice have on our daily lives?

12. **ASK A FEW:** As leaders, we may never be asked to lay down our lives in sacrifice, but what are some sacrifices we'll have to make as leaders in order to show love to those in our ministry and community?

13. **AROUND THE CIRCLE:** Exactly what will you do when we return home from this leadership retreat that will demonstrate your love and sacrifice for others?

TAKEAWAY

Finish up by saying, **The story of Hart's War is powerful and moving. To think that Col. McNamara would return to a POW camp to save his men, knowing he would be executed—that's an awesome sacrifice! However, his story pales in comparison to the sacrifice of Jesus—willing to exchange his life for ours. He was willing to die so we could live.**

As leaders I hope you now have a better understanding of sacrifice. At the very least, I hope you understand that you'll have to make sacrifices for those who follow you. Sometimes that means being inconvenienced, and sometimes it means laying down your life. Regardless, I hope you're willing to sacrifice your plans, your stuff, and yourself for others.

Because of McNamara's sacrifice, his men got to live; because of Jesus' sacrifice, we get eternal life. What will our youth group and church community receive from your sacrifice?

Close in prayer. Give each teen a chance to pray about how she'll lead a sacrificial life as a leader.

[This idea is based on a piece of curriculum written by Todd Pearage for www.thesource4ym.com.]

Share Your Thoughts

With the Author: Your comments will be forwarded to
the author when you send them to *zauthor@zondervan.com*.

With Zondervan: Submit your review of this book
by writing to *zreview@zondervan.com*.

Free Online Resources at
www.zondervan.com

Zondervan AuthorTracker: Be notified whenever your favorite
authors publish new books, go on tour, or post an update
about what's happening in their lives at www.zondervan.com/
authortracker.

Daily Bible Verses and Devotions: Enrich your life with daily
Bible verses or devotions that help you start every morning
focused on God. Visit www.zondervan.com/newsletters.

Free Email Publications: Sign up for newsletters on Christian
living, academic resources, church ministry, fiction, children's
resources, and more. Visit www.zondervan.com/newsletters.

Zondervan Bible Search: Find and compare Bible passages in
a variety of translations at www.zondervanbiblesearch.com.

Other Benefits: Register yourself to receive online benefits
like coupons and special offers, or to participate in research.

ZONDERVAN.com/
AUTHORTRACKER
follow your favorite authors